The *50 plus*®
Guide to
Retirement
Investing

The *50 plus*® Guide to Retirement Investing

Walter W. David

DOW JONES-IRWIN
Homewood, Illinois 60430

To my wife, Lynnette, and children, Brad, Doug, and Elizabeth, for their extra measure of patience during the writing of this book.

50 Plus® is a registered trademark of Retirement Living Publications, Inc., a division of Whitney Communications Company.

© DOW JONES-IRWIN, 1987

ISBN 0-87094-951-9

Library of Congress Catalog Card No. 86–71895

Printed in the United States of America

1 2 3 4 5 6 7 8 9 0 K 4 3 2 1 0 9 8 7

During the retirement years, it can accurately be said that the quality of your life might just very well depend on the quality of your investments. Making proper investments after your retirement is probably more important than at any other time in your life. After all, it is the results of those investments that will produce the income that will pay for your standard of living.

Unfortunately, most people retire from investing when they retire from their active work life. They no longer aggressively seek the best possible investment returns. Widows especially find this a difficult period because they have often not had the opportunity to practice during the earning years.

Making conservative, safe investments does not mean that you have to settle for inferior investment results. You have probably spent a whole career working hard for your money. Now it is time to make your money work hard for you. During your retirement years, you cannot afford to become passive about your investments. The results of those investments during this period of your life are far too important.

The investment world is changing too quickly. During the last five years, we have had inflation from a low of 3 percent to a high of 14 percent and interest rates ranging from 8 percent to a high of 20 percent. Investors who remained aware of the opportunities were able to obtain tremendous benefits. Those who sat idly on the sidelines were forced to accept a lower standard of living and, in some cases, became dependent on family or government programs for financial support.

As a financial planner for the last 14 years, I have found that people entering their retirement years recognize the need to obtain superior investments results. Unfortunately, few financial planners specialize in the needs of the retired person. There is lots of information on how to get rich quick (or lose it quick), but little, if any, information to help the conservative investor obtain the highest rate of return while still maintaining the safety of principal.

The *50 Plus® Guide to Retirement Investing* was written to provide that information. It will help you plan your investments so you can obtain more safety, proper diversification, and the highest return. It will explain:

- Where to get the highest rate of return.
- How to select low risk investments without sacrificing high yield.
- How to reduce your taxes.
- Where to get expert personal investment advice.
- How to maximize the results of your pension plan and social security benefits.
- The fundamentals of proper estate planning.

It is not just a book designed to provide facts. I have provided a number of worksheets and explanations to help you work through your personal investment situation.

After one of the original manned space flights in the early 1960s, the astronauts were invited to testify before a Senate panel. One of the astronauts was asked a hypothetical question. "If during your space flight the light went on indicating an emergency which meant that you had only 60 seconds remaining in your life support system, what would you do?" The astronaut answered, "I would spend 50 seconds thinking and 10 seconds acting." This is excellent advice for investors also. The results of your investments during your retirement years are far too important to treat lightly. Careful planning and prudent investments are essential. The results will affect your standard of living for the rest of your life.

Walter W. David

CONTENTS

CHAPTER ONE

The Continuing Need for Superior Investment Results

I know it seems that you have always been saving and investing for something, right? First the car, then the house, then the kids' college educations, and when nothing else was left, finally you saved and invested for your retirement. Now all of a sudden, as if it crept up on you, you are retired. You have entered one of the most planned-for, dreamed-about, most anticipated parts of your life. You have fewer schedules to keep and more free time. As you begin to grasp the implications of all these changes, it is important that you continue to be an active investor.

The investment decisions that you make today may determine your ability to realize your retirement dreams and set the course for the rest of your life. That may be a very long time. Life expectancy is increasing every year. If you are 65 years old and a man, you will probably be around for another 15 years. If you are a woman, it will probably be a good deal longer. Proper financial planning at this stage of your life could determine the standard of living you will enjoy for the rest of your life. There is a clear and favorable relationship between financial planning, financial security, and good health. Those people who feel financially secure because of proper planning live longer and healthier lives.

Successful investment results have probably never been more important. The number one objective of most retirees is the ability to maintain their life-style. In hundreds of interviews, retired investors have told me that it is very important that they remain independent and never become a burden on anyone else. Unfortunately, only a minority of the American population is able to achieve this goal. In order to maintain your desired life-style, it is important that you continue to generate an income.

THREE SOURCES OF INCOME

Once you have retired, your major sources of income are social security, possibly a pension, and the results of your investments. While there is a lot of talk about the insolvency of the social security system, I'm sure the benefits will continue to be provided for those who are currently retired or those close to retirement. What is in question is the ability of the social security system to continue paying the cost of living adjustments. If the cost of living adjustments should be eliminated, your social security benefits will become "fixed." That simply means that as inflation causes your cost of living to increase, your social security benefits will not keep up.

If you receive a pension, your benefits are almost always fixed, which, like social security, would mean that you receive the same amount each month. These benefits usually do not increase with the cost of living. Some pension plans do have some form of cost of living adjustments, but most do not.

Any potential for increases in your pension and social security are out of your control. They are up to the whims of Congress or are already built into your pension plan. The results of your investments, on the other hand, are very much up to you. Since it is the only element of your income that you can now control, those results are extremely important. The remainder of the book will discuss how to successfully invest your money, what pitfalls to watch out for, and describe many of the investments that you may want to make now that you're retired.

TWO INVESTMENT ENEMIES: TAXES AND INFLATION

One of the major barriers to successful investing is income tax. When 20 percent, 30 percent, or 35 percent of your investment return is taken away in income taxes, it's often difficult to make ends meet on what's left. It is, therefore, very important to consider the implication on your income taxes when selecting the proper investments. There are some investments that can help reduce the amount of taxes that you pay.

Inflation is the other major enemy of successful investing. Inflation's attack on your investments is not so obvious as income taxes', but its effects are just as devastating. Let's take a look at an example.

If you were to invest $10,000 in a money market fund yielding 7 percent, you would receive $700 a year in interest. Now, let's see what a 30 percent tax bracket and a 5 percent inflation rate do to these investment results. First you must pay Uncle Sam $210 in taxes (30% × $700 = $210). Inflation attacks not only your interest but also your principal. Your $10,000 is only worth 95 percent of its value at the end of the year. Subtract $500 ($10,000 × 5% = $500) to account for the effect of inflation. That leaves you with a net annual *loss* of $10 ($700 − $210 − $500 = − $10). That's right, after letting your money work for an entire year, not spending $1 of the interest, you end up losing $10. In the later chapters, we will discuss ways to overcome these two investment enemies.

HOW SAFE IS SAFE?

The most important objective of most investors is safety. What is safety? Is it just investing your money so that your principal is protected against loss? No! It really goes much deeper than that. It is not your money that you want to protect, it's what your money will purchase that needs protecting. Take the concept one step further. You really want to protect the life-style and independence paid for by the income generated by your investments. So safety means the protection of the buying power of your principal and the return it generates. If the value of your investments is not increasing at the rate of inflation, you are actually losing money. Does this mean that you should go out and make high-risk investments in order to stay ahead of inflation? No. It does mean that you need to take a look at the broader picture of safety when you make your investments. Far too many investors feel that they have done a good job by placing their money in institutions that guarantee that their original investment will be returned.

The following illustrates the yearly return on a $100,000 investment that has a seven-year maturity. Review the results and see what you think:

Year 1: Receive $5,357.
Year 2: Receive $4,905.
Year 3: Receive $4,492.
Year 4: Receive $4,114.
Year 5: Receive $3,767.
Year 6: Receive $3,450.
Year 7: Receive $3,159 plus $54,005 = $57,164.
Total received: $83,249.

No, not plus $100,000; that's all you get back, $83,249. Sound good, sound safe; invest $100,000 to receive $83,249? No, of course not! These are the inflation-adjusted, after-tax returns for an investor in a 35 percent tax bracket who, in 1977, invested in a seven-year certificate of deposit (CD) paying 9 percent interest. During this period, inflation averaged 9.2 percent. So much for safety.

WHAT'S THE POINT?

Over the years, I have seen many people do an excellent job of investing their money to provide for retirement. They would work hard to search out the best investments that offered superior returns. But, when they retired from active employment, they also retired from investing. Unfortunately, their job was only half done.

In all probability, you have more investable dollars right now than you have ever had before. In many cases, you have sold larger homes to move into smaller ones and sold businesses that took a lifetime to build. You are faced with investment choices that you have not faced before. The number of investments from which to choose can be mind-boggling. You realize that you can't afford to make a mistake. If you goof now, there is no opportunity to start over. You have spent a lifetime working hard for your money. It is now time to get your money working as hard as possible for you. Successful investing takes time, effort, and energy, but it can also be fun. The information in the rest of this book will help you select the proper investments that will suit your individual needs and help provide your desired retirement life-style.

SUMMARY

1. When you retire from working, you can't retire from investing.
2. In retirement, your three main sources of income are pension, social security, and investment income.
3. When making investments, first evaluate the possible effect of inflation and taxes.
4. Safety is the protection of the buying power of your investment income.

CHAPTER TWO

Inflation: A Two-Edged Sword

Each time, the calculator registered the same number. It seemed to Helen that each month the money would run out a little bit sooner. She and her husband John budgeted very closely. Over the last few years they had cut back all unnecessary expenses, but now she was not able to make ends meet. What had happened? When they retired eight years ago, they felt comfortable with their financial preparation for retirement. They had not been extravagant; in fact, their spending had remained according to their long-term plan. There were no long-term illnesses, no big expenses, no special situations to account for it. At first, they were saving just a little less each month. Then not saving anything at all. Now, even with all the cutbacks, they just were not able to make ends meet. She had really never given any thought to inflation before. Even now, she didn't understand what caused it. She wasn't sure the experts did. It was almost like a cancer, she thought. It starts quietly, imperceptibly, almost without notice; then all of a sudden, one day you find yourself in deep trouble.

WHAT IS INFLATION?

If you were responsible for making ends meet from 1973 to 1980, you know what inflation is. In case you missed it, inflation is when the price of almost everything goes up. For the retired person it may cause expenses to be rising faster than income.

Inflation is now a fact of life for Americans. Most experts cannot agree on what causes it, and they are definitely not in agreement on how to cure it. In fact, they can't even agree on whether it is good or bad. The cancer of inflation is, right now, in remission. But whether inflation continues at a reduced level or comes raging back, you don't have to be held captive by its ravages. There are two sides to inflation. While some are hurt by it, others are actually helped and benefited financially from inflation. The important thing to understand is how to position yourself to benefit from inflation and to protect yourself during your retirement years. The solutions are easy if you understand them. Why are so many retired people hurt by inflation? The reasons are numerous. They involve a lack of information, procrastination, and fear. The facts are these. Inflation will continue to be a problem for a long time to come. If you plan for it, by selecting the proper kinds of investments, you can avoid its destructive impact. In order to make the proper investment selections, it's important that you understand the two major kinds of investments.

TWO KINDS OF INVESTMENTS

With 14 years in the investment business, I still don't have a crystal ball that will accurately predict the future. In fact, in those 14 years I've never met anybody or heard of anybody who has one. But if we did have a crystal ball that could accurately predict the future and that crystal ball told us we were going to have a high rate of inflation for the next five years, what kinds of investments would you want to make? You would certainly want to be in things like real estate, some kinds of growth-oriented common stocks, gold, silver, platinum, and other precious metals, antiques, coins, and fine art; those investments that benefit from inflation. Why do these investments benefit from inflation? Remember, inflation causes the price of things to increase. If you own a house and the price of other houses is increasing, yours will also. Therefore, the value of the investment you own is increasing. The same would be true for the other investments mentioned above.

What do all these investments have in common? In each case, you own the asset. You own the real estate, the common stocks, the gold, the silver, the antiques, the coins, or whatever. One major form of investment is through ownership. In each case, the investments mentioned earlier are things you own. In inflationary periods, you want to be invested in assets that you own because the price and the value of these assets is increasing.

Now, if you looked into the crystal ball and it told you that we were going to have very low or no inflation over the next five years, what kinds of investments would you want to make? You would want to invest in long-term bonds, certificates of deposit and long-term mortgages. The second major way of investing your money is to lend it. If you purchase a bond, you have loaned your money to a municipality, a corporation, or the U.S. government. If you invest in a CD, you have loaned your money to a bank or savings and loan. And, if you invest in a mortgage, you have simply loaned your money to somebody else to purchase a piece of real estate. Why are these investments good when we have low or no inflation? In a low inflation environment, prices are going up very slowly or not at all. In this case, you want your money to be invested where it will pay you a high, stable cash return.

HOW INFLATION HURTS

During high inflationary periods, the prices of almost everything are going up. That means that the dollars that you have to spend are losing their purchasing power. The same $20 bill will not buy as much one year from now as it does today. Since the cost of everything that we need to live is going up, we simply say that during high inflationary periods the cost of living is going up. That means, you must earn more and more each year just to remain at the same standard of living. If inflation is 10 percent, you must earn 10 percent more next year just to stay even.

Now here's the problem. Loan-oriented investments such as bonds, CDs, and mortgages are considered "fixed-income" investments. A fixed-income investment simply pays the same amount each year. The amount won't go up and it won't go down; in other words, it's fixed.

If you invest $10,000 in a certificate of deposit at the bank paying 10 percent per year for five years, they will pay you interest in the amount of $1,000 each year for those five years. No matter what happens to interest rates or the inflation rate, you will receive $1,000 each year. In other words, the amount that you will receive is fixed, and therein lies the problem. If you need to receive 10 percent more each year just to maintain the same standard of living, but the amount that you receive from your investments is fixed, you start falling behind. Inflation causes the buying power of the income from fixed-income investments to be worth less each year.

Inflation has another trick to play on the fixed-income investment. Remember your $10,000 investment in the certificate of deposit? At the end of the five-year term, you will receive your $10,000 back. Unfortunately, because of inflation, that $10,000 will not buy nearly as much as it did the day you deposited it.

How does inflation hurt the retiree? It causes your cost of living to increase, thereby requiring that you generate more income each year just to remain even. In addition, it causes the buying power of your principal to decrease.

THE BENEFITS FROM INFLATION

As the title of this chapter implies, there is a benefit to inflation. Whether you benefit depends on the kind of investments that you have made. If you have invested your money in things that you own, inflation will reward you. These kinds of investments are known as "growth investments." Growth investments increase in value as the prices of everything else increase.

As an example, let's assume that you purchase a $50,000 house for cash and you rent that house to somebody else for $5,000 a year. Since you have purchased the house for all cash, you can use the full rental income for living expenses. If inflation is causing the cost of living to go up at 10 percent a year, it's probable that you will be able to raise the rents 10 percent each year. That means in the second year you will receive $5,500 in rent. Therefore, as inflation causes your cost of living to go up, the income that you receive from your growth investment also goes up to provide you with the additional income.

In addition to increasing income from your growth investment, the value of that investment is increasing also. At the end of the first year, the home you purchased for $50,000 will probably be worth $55,000. Therefore, with the value of the home increasing each year, the value of your principal maintains its full purchasing power, even with inflation.

THE EARNING YEARS

During your earning years, inflation was not a major problem. Take a look at Figure 2–1 and you will see why. The dashed line at the bottom indicates expenses during your earning years. Notice that they rise over the years. Part of that increase depicts an increased standard of living and part is caused by inflation. Increasing expenses did not present a major problem because your income was also going up. It was increasing, in part, because as an employee you were becoming more valuable. It was also increasing because inflation was causing general wages and prices to increase. During your earning years, if you did a good job of budgeting and lived within your budget, you could always save some money. Inflation, while it did exist, was not as noticeable.

Remember, we talked about the three sources of income during retirement years: your pension, social security, and your investments. If all three sources of income were fixed income, your situation might look like Figure 2–2. Look at the income line at the top. It's flat. This illustrates a situation when income is totally fixed. It doesn't increase or decrease over the years. In this example, it is $24,000 a year. This would not be a problem if expenses also remained fixed. In this chart, we have drawn a straight line for expenses at $19,000 a year. This situation assumes that there is no inflation and you continue to enjoy your current life-style without any increases in expenses. In addition, you are able to save

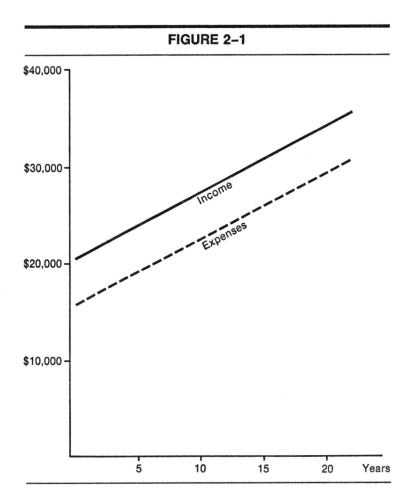

FIGURE 2–1

$5,000 a year. Unfortunately, this does not depict the real world in which we live.

Now look at Figure 2–3. Again, notice that your income is fixed at $24,000 a year. But in this situation, expenses are increasing because of inflation. In Year 1, you are able to save $5,000. Look what happens by Year 4. Your expenses begin to exceed your income. What do you do? (I've asked the same question in many of my seminars. My favorite answer comes from a gentleman in Melbourne, Florida, who said, "You start to sweat.") While sweating may be a natural reaction, it will not solve the problem. It may mean that you have to start

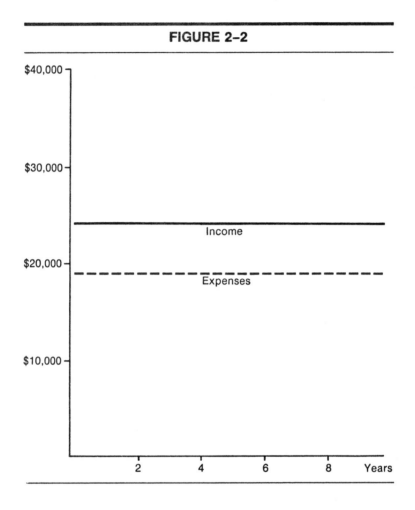

FIGURE 2–2

cutting back on your life-style, giving up some of the things that you had planned for during your retirement years. It may mean that you begin spending some of your principal. Spending your principal is not all bad. After all, it's your money and you worked hard to save it. (You told your children that you are going to spend their inheritance anyway.) But, if you start using up your principal, you are really using up your source of income. For every dollar worth of principal you spend, there is one less dollar you have to invest to generate a continuous flow of income. What is the solution?

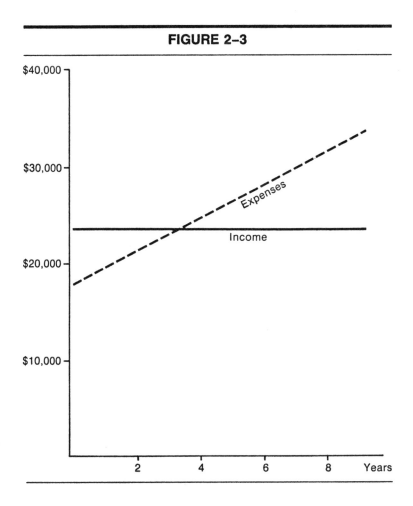

FIGURE 2–3

MAXIMIZE YOUR INVESTMENT INCOME

While you cannot control the fixed nature of your pension and social security income, your investment income is a different story. That is under your control. Unfortunately, most retirees make investments that generate only fixed income. We have already seen the effects of inflation on these kinds of investments, but let me drive home the point one more time. Referring to Figure 2–3, assume that inflation is averaging 7.7 percent a year. This is approximately the average between 1970 and 1982. Assume further that your income is $24,000 a year and that your living expenses are $19,000 a year. It would take just three years before your expenses exceeded your income and you would be forced to cut back on your life-style. In only seven years, your living expenses would be almost $32,000 a year. If your income had remained fixed at $24,000, you would have a real problem. To avoid that problem you must maximize your investment income. Let's take a look at some ways of doing that.

Seek the Highest Return

The most obvious solution is to always seek the highest rate of return while maintaining your safety. To do this, you must look beyond the obvious and most convenient investments to seek the ones that will give you the most income. Instead of investing in a certificate of deposit at the bank, consider purchasing a government security, like a Ginnie Mae (Government National Mortgage Association), which will be discussed in a later chapter.

Currently, you can get almost two percentage points greater income investing in a Ginnie Mae without sacrificing safety. In addition, by making investments that are somewhat longer term, you can substantially increase the income you receive without sacrificing a great deal of safety. Notice in Figure 2–4 that if you increase your income you can put off the time at which a problem might occur for several years.

Reduce Taxes

Obviously, the smaller your tax bill, the more money you will have to spend. There are a number of investments like municipal bonds and some types of real estate that provide you with tax-free income. Without having to pay current income taxes, your spendable income increases. With this additional income you could put off the inevitable problem another several years. Be sure to read the section carefully on tax benefits. Investments that have tax advantages are not necessarily for everyone.

FIGURE 2–4

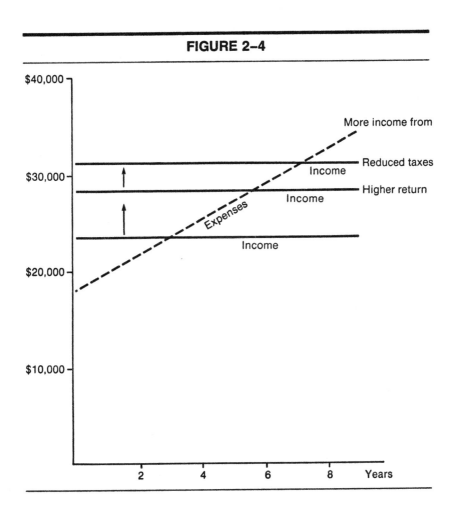

Make Your Income Grow

Remember we discussed that inflation is not all bad. For every loser to inflation, there is also a winner. During inflationary periods if you are an owner of houses, investment real estate, antiques, common stocks, or other investments, you actually benefit from inflation. The long-term solution is to have some of your money invested in ownership. You want to have the right mix of fixed income investments to pay you a

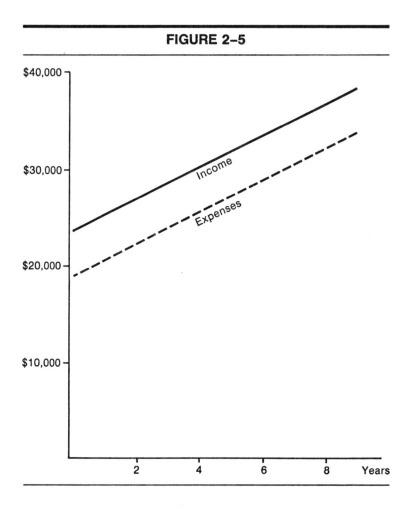

FIGURE 2–5

high return as well as growth-oriented investments to keep you up with inflation. By doing so, your situation may be depicted in Figure 2–5. Just like during your earning years, your income is increasing so the effects of inflation are not damaging.

GOLDMAN SACHS STUDY

Let's take one more look at the effects of inflation on investments in Figure 2–6. This chart indicates the results of a study done by Goldman Sachs between July 31, 1970, and

FIGURE 2-6

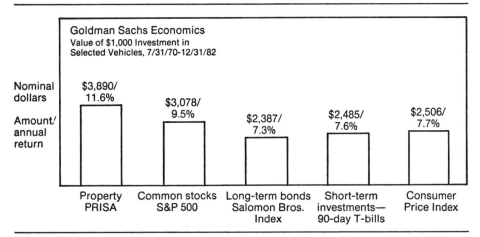

Goldman Sachs Economics
Value of $1,000 Investment in
Selected Vehicles, 7/31/70-12/31/82

Nominal dollars

Amount/ annual return

$3,890/ 11.6%
Property PRISA

$3,078/ 9.5%
Common stocks S&P 500

$2,387/ 7.3%
Long-term bonds Salomon Bros. Index

$2,485/ 7.6%
Short-term investments— 90-day T-bills

$2,506/ 7.7%
Consumer Price Index

SOURCE: Leon G. Cooperman, Steven G. Einhorn, and Meyer Melnikoff, "Our Expanding Universe: The Case for Pension Fund Investment in Property," Topical Paper, June 1983.

December 31, 1982. During that period inflation (as measured by the consumer price index [CPI]) averaged 7.7 percent a year. As you can see, investments in short-term Treasury bills and in long-term bonds (loans) both lost ground to inflation. If you were a retiree and invested in long-term bonds during that time, the income you received would not have kept up with the rate of inflation. Worse yet, the value of the principal will purchase less than half of what it would have the day you made the deposit.

On the other hand, take a look at what happened to investors who owned something, like common stocks as represented by the Standard & Poor's 500 index or real estate as represented by the Prudential Life Insurance index of real estate holdings. In both cases, investors would not only have kept up with inflation but actually benefited from the increase in the value of their assets.

What conclusions can you draw from this? It does not mean that you should go liquidate all your bonds and CDs and rush out and plunge into the stock market. You should, however, recognize that inflation may be with us for a long time and must be considered when you make your investments. You must investigate a wide variety of investment opportunities to be sure that you are getting the highest rate possible.

In the next chapter you will meet Bill and Susan Retiree and find out how they planned for their retirement. You will have a chance to see what problems and opportunities they encountered and what action they took.

SUMMARY

1. Consider the effects of inflation when making your investments.
2. Be sure that you understand the tax implications of the investments that you make.
3. Seek out the highest rate of return while maintaining a high level of safety.
4. The most convenient investment may not be the best.

Before You Invest

Bill and Susan had worked hard. They tried to do the best job they could at planning and saving during their earning years. But this was it. The earning years were over. They hoped to be able to enjoy the rest of their lives with the life-style they had planned, but they just weren't sure. They had received so much conflicting information from friends, relatives, neighbors, books, and tapes. How should they invest the nest egg they had worked so hard for and depended upon to support them for the rest of their lives? They just didn't want to make a mistake. But what about the unknowns? What about an extended illness? What about inflation? What if they lived to be 110? How could they plan for all those things? They decided that the first step was to visit a financial planner.

PLAN AHEAD

Many football coaches would tell you football games are won or lost depending on how well the team is prepared. Having the right game plan can mean the difference between success and failure. Just as in football, proper planning is the most important step to successful investing. Planning is much more important than any single investment that you will ever make.

Financial planning is much like planning for a long trip. You must decide ahead of time where you are going and what you will need to get there. In practical terms, this means you must decide what kind of life-style you will want during your retirement. Next, you should establish a budget to find out what it will cost. Finally, you must evaluate your income sources to see if you can afford it.

PLAN TOGETHER

The planning process can be very exciting. If you're married, be sure your spouse reads this book. This is a great opportunity for both of you to work together and learn together. After all, the investment objectives you are seeking to achieve are joint objectives. Men, this is a great chance to make up for some lost opportunities. Most guys go through their earning years making all the investment decisions for their family. They often fail to involve their wives in the investment decision-making process. The cost of not allowing them to participate and learn can be devastating. The chances are very good that your wife is going to outlive you. How can you expect her to make the correct investment choices after you are gone if she never had the opportunity to learn or to practice? You have some time now. The pressures of day-to-day business are over. Be sure that you use this time to involve her.

Wives, half the responsibility is yours. You have to take the time and show the interest. You have to do the reading and attend the seminars. You are perfectly capable of learning all there is to know about the investments you make. When you make a new investment, write out the check to the investment company. Actually talk to the banker, stock broker, or financial planner who will be handling the investment for you. You place the order and deposit the income checks as they come in. An investment of a little time and energy now can pay big dividends later on. Besides, making money can be a lot of fun.

Think of this process of re-evaluating your investments as an exercise. Physical exercise makes you feel better and probably helps you live longer. Well, financial exercise can do the same thing. Statistically, those who do a good job of financial planning for their retirement years live longer. In addition, because of the good planning and the increased income, the quality of their lives can also be much better.

One of the best methods of learning is through illustration. Therefore, I want to introduce you to Bill and Susan Retiree. We are going to follow their investment process throughout the book. This will give you an opportunity to see a real-life example of how one couple successfully planned their investments for their retirement years.

BACKGROUND INFORMATION ON BILL AND SUSAN RETIREE

Bill and Susan, both age 63, came to Florida from New York in 1984 after Bill's retirement. They sold their home on Long Island, used some of the proceeds to pay off all of their debts, and paid cash for a new $78,000 home.

They planned a long time for their retirement, and they want to be sure to invest their money so that they can realize their retirement dreams. Bill and Susan are in a bowling league together and Bill plays three rounds of golf a week with friends. They enjoy traveling and plan to return to Long Island once a year to visit. In addition, they plan one short cruise each year and have several three-day trips planned with their golf club. Bill and Susan have done a thorough job of budgeting for all their reasonable expenses. They feel they will be able to save some money each year. However, they are very concerned about the possibility of increased inflation or the financial effects of a long-term major illness.

They receive $4,910 a year in pension benefits and $9,864 a year in social security benefits. Bill and Susan worked hard to save for their retirement. They have investments of $136,000. Most of their investments are in fixed-income assets such as certificates of deposit, savings account, government bonds, and annuities. They have a small amount invested in a stock mutual fund for growth.

Their retirement needs are modest and they are quite satisfied with the life-style that they will have. They would like to leave an estate to their children, but that is not a major priority. Their most important concern is remaining independent for as long as they live and never becoming a financial burden on their family.

WHAT YOU WILL NEED: THE BUDGET

Many years ago there was a very wise king. He wanted to give his people something of lasting value. He called his scribes and wise men and gave them an order, "Go throughout the world seeking all knowledge, write it down, and bring it back to me." They searched the world gathering all knowledge. They wrote it down in 12 big volumes and brought it back to the king. After reading every word, he determined that the books did contain all the knowledge in the world but, being a wise king, he knew that his people would not take the time to read 12 large volumes. He called back his scribes and wise men and told them to condense it. As commanded, they reduced it to one large volume. After reading the volume and concluding again that it contained all the knowledge in the world, he asked them to condense it further. They came back this time with one chapter and, once again, he sent them back to condense it further. They came back with one page, then one paragraph, and finally at his command, they brought back one sentence. As the king unwrapped the scroll with the one sentence written on it, a big smile came across his face. All the scribes and wise men breathed a sigh of relief. He would finally accept it. The king read the sentence and he knew that all the knowledge in the world was truly compiled and condensed into that one sentence. The sentence read, "There ain't no free lunch."

That story has many applications in real life. It will take a little effort to financially insure your hopes and dreams during your retirement years. After all, those vacations and golf outings are going to cost something. The next important step in your planning process is to find out exactly how much. That's right. You're going to have to do a budget.

Generally speaking, your expenses are going to drop about 25 percent after you retire. You won't have to buy as many clothes, your commuting costs will decrease and, yes,

---

TABLE 3-1

Fixed expenses	
House payment	0
Total fixed	0
Variable expenses	
Utilities	$ 1,800
Food	3,500
Clothing	1,000
Income taxes	1,850
Property taxes	800
Transportation	2,100
Medical	1,000
Debt repayment	0
Maintenance	500
Insurance	900
Vacations	2,400
Contributions	1,000
Gifts	1,000
Furnishings	500
Other	1,000
Total variable	$19,350
Total expenses	$19,350

---

finally, your tax bracket will come down. Before you begin your budget, let's take a look at the budget that Bill and Susan developed for their retirement years.

Table 3-1 shows the results of their budgeting process. If you will remember, Bill and Susan had purchased their home for all cash; therefore, they do not have a house payment or any other fixed expenses. When filling out your budget, fixed expenses are those that will not change over a long period of time. The most common fixed expense would be your house payment. It is fixed because you know that the house payment will remain the same despite the effects of inflation. If you are renting, however, rent payments would not be fixed because, as inflation goes up, so will your rent. Other fixed expenses may include payments for life insurance policies that remain level or long-term mortgages on other property. Car payments are variable expenses. When a car is paid off in two or three years, it's probable that you will buy another one. Your car payment will go up because the price of your new car will have increased due to inflation.

All of Bill and Susan's expenses are variable. Variable expenses are those that will rise with inflation. Bill and Susan have budgeted and feel that they can live the life-style that they desire on $19,350 a year. Because all of their expenses are variable, they will all be going up at approximately the same rate as inflation. If inflation runs at the rate of 10 percent a year, their living expenses will increase by $1,935 that year.

The budgeting process can really be a very healthy, goal-setting opportunity. By budgeting, you can ensure that the things you want most receive top priority. It provides an excellent opportunity for the retired couple to sit down together and discuss these priorities. You have been together 30, 40, maybe 50 years or more; don't worry, your marriage will withstand this. In order to get the things you want most in your retirement years, it's very important to agree on what they are and then budget for them. If you have not done a budget, you can use the same categories that Bill and Susan used. Be sure to keep your fixed and variable expenses separate. A budget worksheet is provided in the Appendix.

HOW TO DETERMINE YOUR INCOME

If you have already retired, you probably know what you get from social security and what you will be receiving from your pension plan. If you have not retired, this is an important part of the planning process. If you work for a corporation that has a pension plan, you can find out exactly what you will receive and when you will receive it from your pension benefits department. An income worksheet is provided in the Appendix.

SOCIAL SECURITY

There has been a lot of publicity in the last few years about the potential failure of the social security system and about its inability to pay out benefits to those people who have paid

TABLE 3–2
Table of Retirement Benefits at Age 65
(for workers who reach age 65 in 1987)

If Your Average Indexed Yearly Earnings Were:	Workers at 65 Collect Every Month	You and Your Spouse Age 65 Collect
$ 1,200	$ 93.10	$ 139.60
3,000	232.80	349.20
5,000	298.10	447.10
8,000	380.90	571.30
10,000	436.20	654.30
12,000	491.40	737.10
14,000	546.50	819.70
16,000	601.80	902.70
18,000	657.00	985.50
20,000	702.50	1,053.70
22,000	728.40	1,092.60
25,000	767.20	1,150.80

in for so many years. The facts are that with recent changes, the social security system is in excellent condition. It is estimated that in 1986, $196 billion in benefits will be paid out to over 40 million people. It is probable that your social security benefits will provide a significant portion of your retirement income. If you are about ready to retire, you are going to want to know how much your social security benefits will be.

Estimating your exact social security benefit is somewhat complicated. It depends on how long you have paid into the social security system and what amounts you have paid in. Table 3–2 below can provide you with a good estimate of what you can expect from social security.

RETIRING BEFORE 65

It is not necessary that you wait until age 65 to collect your social security benefits. It is possible to collect those benefits as early as age 62. You should be aware that if you choose to begin collecting your benefits early that you will receive a lesser amount. You will receive a lesser amount because you will be receiving that benefit longer. If you choose to retire at age 62, you will get approximately 80 percent of your age 65 benefits. If you begin collecting at age 63, you will receive 86²/₃ percent of the amount you would have received at age 65. If you wait until you reach age 64, the amount received will be 93¹/₃ percent of your normal benefits due at 65.

WORKING WHILE RECEIVING SOCIAL SECURITY BENEFITS

The social security regulations allow you to earn income up to certain limits while still receiving your maximum social security benefits. The amounts that you are allowed to receive in earnings depend upon your age. In 1986, those between the ages of 65 and 70 could earn $7,800 without loss of benefits while those under age 65 could earn $5,760. Those amounts will rise in future years based on the level of inflation.

It is also possible for you to earn more than these limits listed and still receive some portion of your social security benefits. The more you earn, the smaller amount of social security benefits you will receive. If you earn more than the $7,800 limit, $1 in benefits will be deducted for each $2 in earnings above the $7,800. Starting in 1990, $1 in benefits will be deducted for each $3 in earnings above the exempt amount.

You can find out approximately how much you will be receiving from social security by simply filing Form SSA-7004. You can get the form from your local social security office. Fill it out. It's short and requires no special instructions. In about six weeks you should receive a printout from the Social Security Administration. This will provide a history of your earnings from all employers from the years that you have worked. From this you will be able to determine what your social security benefit will be at age 62 and after. If you have any problems, the Social Security Administration is willing to help.

If you have never filled out Form SSA-7004 (see Figure 3-1), you ought to do it. Believe it or not, even the federal government occasionally makes a mistake. If there has been a mistake and you have not been credited for all your years of service, the statute of limitations period is 3 years 3 months,

FIGURE 3–1
Social Security Form SSA-7004

FOLD HERE & STAPLE OR TAPE TO CLOSE

REQUEST FOR STATEMENT OF EARNINGS
(PLEASE PRINT IN INK OR USE TYPEWRITER)

FOR SSA USE ONLY	
AX	
SP	

I REQUEST A SUMMARY STATEMENT OF EARNINGS FROM MY SOCIAL SECURITY RECORD

NH
Full name you use in work or business

First	Middle Initial	Last

SN
Social security number shown on your card

Your date of birth
DB | Month | Day | Year | **A**

MA
Other Social Security number(s) you have used

Your Sex
SX ☐ Male ☐ Female

AK
Other name(s) you have used (include your maiden name)

FOLD HERE

PRIVACY STATEMENT

The Social Security Administration (SSA) is authorized to collect information asked on this form under section 205 of the Social Security Act. It is needed so SSA can quickly identify your record and prepare the earnings statement you requested. While you are not required to furnish the information, failure to do so may prevent your request from being processed. The information will be used primarily for issuing your earnings statement.

I am the individual to whom the record pertains. I understand that if I knowingly and willingly request or receive a record about an individual under false pretenses I would be guilty of a Federal crime and could be fined up to $5000.

Sign your name here: (Do not print) | Date

I AUTHORIZE YOU TO SEND THE STATEMENT TO THE NAME AND ADDRESS BELOW: *(To be completed in all cases)*

PN
Name of the addressee

AD
Street number and name

City and state | **ZP** | Zip Code

Form SSA-7004 PC   OP 1   (4-84) Previous Editions are Obsolete

---

and 15 days. That simply means that if you don't get them corrected within that period of time, you will not get credit for them. The burden of correcting these problems is on you, not the government. You should check on your social security credits at least once every two years prior to retirement.

YOUR PENSION BENEFIT

During your earning years, you may have accrued a rather substantial pension benefit. Upon retirement you may be faced with a choice of how to take that benefit. You may be offered a guaranteed income for the rest of your life or you may have the opportunity to remove all the funds in one lump sum. You should be aware that any pension benefit is fully taxable with the exception of any money that you contributed to the pension plan that was already taxed.

If you have been enrolled in your pension plan for at least five years, you will be eligible to withdraw your funds under the 10-year averaging method. This allows you to remove all the funds in your pension plan in one lump sum but to be taxed at a lower rate. Your taxes are calculated as if you were a single taxpayer and had no exemptions or standard deductions. Your taxable income is equal to 10 percent of your total lump sum payment. The actual tax calculated is then multiplied by 10 and this is the amount owed to the IRS. As an example, assume in 1984 that you took a $100,000 payout from your pension. Your tax base for calculation is $2,300 plus 10 percent of $100,000 or $12,300. From Schedule X for single taxpayers, you find that the tax is $1,473. Multiply $1,473 times 10. This would indicate a $14,730 tax payment is due. You now have $100,000 minus $14,730 to reinvest. This example ignores any savings or contributions made before 1974. Your actual tax may be lower on those amounts as distributions will be taxed as long-term capital gains.

You may also choose to take a cash payment from your pension and "roll" it into a self-directed IRA. As long as you put the money into the IRA within 60 days of withdrawal from your pension, you will not be taxed. The funds remain in the IRA and accumulate tax-free. When you withdraw the funds from the IRA, you will be taxed at your ordinary income tax rate. As with any IRA, you must begin withdrawing funds at age 70½.

The way in which you take your pension benefits is entirely up to you. Many people prefer the opportunity of the lump sum distribution because they then control their money and might better be able to provide for a surviving spouse. Many pension benefits now provide only 55 percent of the pension benefit to be paid to a surviving spouse. It is important to make the way you take your pension benefits work smoothly with the rest of your financial planning.

WHAT TO DO WITH YOUR IRA

Once you have retired, what should you do with your IRA? First of all, be sure that it is receiving the highest yield possible. You may find that you have accumulated your IRA at a bank or savings and loan for convenience purposes where the rates have not been competitive with other investments. If you find that this is the case, you may consider a self-directed IRA. A self-directed IRA, just like the name implies, allows you to invest your IRA money in a wider variety of investments. Most stock brokerage firms and large insurance companies make available self-directed IRAs. Remember, your IRA investment is just like any other part of your portfolio and should fit with the rest of the investments.

Secondly, you will want to defer taking any money out of your IRA for as long as possible. When you remove money from your IRA to meet living expenses, you are taxed on that income. As long as you can meet living expenses from other sources of income, your IRA investment continues to compound tax-free. At age 70½ you must begin taking some of the capital from your IRA. This must be done based on a schedule provided by the Internal Revenue Service.

Thirdly, if you continue to have a source of earned income, you should continue funding your IRA if you are not yet age 70½. For people between the ages of 59½ and 70½, the IRA is the greatest deal going. If you have earned income, possibly from a part-time job, you can put 100 percent of that income, up to $2,000 a year, into the IRA. By doing this, you will receive a $2,000 tax deduction[1] for the amount invested and the money accumulates tax-free. Should you need to withdraw the funds for an emergency or living expenses, you would have to pay the income taxes, but there is no penalty after age 59½.

---

[1] As this book goes to press, the U.S. Congress is debating the continuation of the IRA deduction.

EVALUATING YOUR INVESTMENTS

Now it's time to take your investment inventory. Remember, you are getting ready to take a long trip. You will want to be sure that you have enough provisions to make it through the trip. Before evaluating your investments, let's take a look at an evaluation for Bill and Susan. As you can see from Table 3–3, Bill and Susan's investments are broken down into the two major categories. They are growth-oriented investments where they own something and fixed-income investments where they have made loans. As you can see from Bill and Susan's example, most of their investments are in fixed income. From those, they receive $11,200 in income, which is an average rate of return of 8.78 percent. A worksheet for evaluating your investments is provided in the Appendix.

Their only growth-oriented investment is from a stock mutual fund. They currently have $8,700 invested in that mutual fund which generates an income for them of $487. Remember from our previous chapter, fixed-income investments are those that are going to provide a steady stream of income that will neither increase nor decrease with inflation. On the other hand, growth-oriented investments provide income that will tend to increase as inflation increases. This will become very important in the next chapter.

YOUR INVESTMENT INVENTORY

Now it's your turn. Use the same categories as Bill and Susan to make your inventory process easier. Separate your investments into fixed and growth. The categories on the illustration will help you. If you are not sure, ask yourself, "Do I own an asset (growth), or have I made a loan (fixed)?" In the case of real estate, if you own the property it's growth. If you hold a mortgage, it's fixed income (you have loaned the money for someone else to buy the property).

To properly categorize mutual funds, you must look at what kind of investments the mutual fund makes. If the mutual fund holds bonds (a bond fund), it is a fixed-income investment. If the fund invests in common stocks, then list it as a common stock under the growth asset category. If this is

TABLE 3-3

Current Fixed Income Allocation

	Amount	Rate	Income
CDs	$ 60,000	8.90%	$ 5,340
Savings account	22,000	7.50	1,650
Money market	15,600	7.20	1,123
Government bonds	7,500	8.50	638
Corporate bonds	0	0.00	0
Municipal bonds	0	0.00	0
Mortgages	0	0.00	0
Annuities	16,500	11.50	1,898
Preferred stock	0	0.00	0
IRA	6,000	9.20	552
Other	0	0.00	0
Total	$127,600	8.78%	$11,200

Current Growth Asset Allocation

	Amount	Rate	Income
Common stocks	$ 8,700	5.60%	$ 487
Oil and gas	0	0.00	0
Real estate	0	0.00	0
IRA	0	0.00	0
Other	0	0.00	0
Total	$ 8,700	5.60%	$ 487

Current Income Situation

	Income
Earned income	$ 0
Pension	4,910
Social security	9,864
Growth income	487
Fixed income	11,200
Total	$26,461

a little confusing at this point, wait until you finish reading the book. The additional information in the later chapters about specific investments will help clarify this for you.

BILL AND SUSAN'S RESULTS

How are Bill and Susan doing? They have indicated total income of $26,461. Their expenses are $19,350 which leaves them $7,111 a year in savings. That looks pretty good today. But how will they be doing 5 or 10 years from now? In Chapter 4 you will learn how to project your income needs and investment return in the future. Before we start predicting the future, it is important to learn to keep records about the past.

RECORD-KEEPING

It is very important to get in the habit of keeping good investment records. At the very least, a good record-keeping system can help show you where you have been. At the worst, not having a good record-keeping system can be very expensive. Millions of dollars are lost each year by people who simply forget about small bank account deposits. After the bank tries to locate the depositor and fails, their money simply reverts to the state. Consider the plight of a new widow who is unable to find her husband's life insurance policies. Even when she finds them, she is never sure that she has found them all because there were no records of what he had or where they were kept.

Take some time to set up a simple inventory of everything that you own and where it's located. Set up a filing system so that if you weren't around, your spouse or relative could find the information they needed. Some of your records could be filed at home. Others should be kept in your safe deposit box. The ones that you keep in your safe deposit box should be those that are valuable or difficult to replace such as birth certificates, stock certificates, bearer bonds, business contracts, and real estate deeds.

SELLING YOUR HOME

Having achieved the age of 55 years has some distinct benefits. One of the best tax benefits is the "over 55 rule." Internal Revenue Code Section 121 allows the seller of a principal residence to exclude up to $125,000 of the profit of the sale of that residence from tax if they are 55 years or older as of the date of the sale. The law is really quite simple and quite an advantage, but there are several things you should know so that you do not accidentally lose that exemption.

1. You must be 55 years or older on the day of the sale. It is not adequate that the seller become 55 years old in the same year as the sale. If the house is held in joint title of husband and wife, it is necessary that only one of them be 55 years or older.
2. It must be your principal place of residence.
3. You must have owned and lived in that place of residence for three of the five years before the sale.
4. You must have never used the "over 55" exemption before.
5. You are only allowed one $125,000 tax exemption per marriage. You cannot claim $125,000 exemption for the husband and then later claim a second $125,000 for the wife.

There is an unusual part of the law that allows $250,000 total tax exemption if two persons over 55 are co-owners but are not married to each other. As an example, if two brothers live together and are both 55 years old or older, they can claim a $250,000 exemption ($125,000 each). If a husband and wife are planning to sell their house because they are getting a divorce, it would be prudent to wait until after the divorce to sell the house. In that way, as nonmarried co-owners, they would get a $125,000 exemption each. Since the rule allows the $125,000 exemption only once in a lifetime, it can have another interesting twist. Suppose Bill and Susan are married, sell their house, and take a $125,000 exemption. Susan later dies, and Bill marries Ann who already owns a home. If Ann later decides to sell her house, she is not entitled to the $125,000 exemption because Bill had already taken his. To keep from losing a $125,000 exemption, Ann might have sold her house prior to marriage.

ROLLING OVER PROFITS

Most older people have owned more than one home. When selling their previous residences, they usually did not pay income tax on the profits because they purchased another house of equal or greater value within two years. As you move closer to retirement and the children have left the nest, a smaller home is often desirable. In this case, it is often not possible to shelter the profit by rolling it over into a home of greater value. This may be an excellent time to use the $125,000 tax exemption. This exemption can be used to shelter all the profits up to $125,000 accumulated in all the previous residences.

Remember, however, that any unused portion of the $125,000 is wasted. If your home profit is only $100,000 upon sale, you are not able to save the unused $25,000 for future use. Naturally, if your home sale only involves a small profit at this time, you may choose to roll that over into your next residence, thus saving your exemption for a later sale when it can be better utilized.

REFINANCING TO INVEST

I am often asked by couples if I think it makes sense to refinance their house, take equity out, and invest that money. For the couple nearing retirement, the answer is almost always "no." The bank or savings and loan lending you money as a mortgage on your house considers it a moderate risk loan. They are going to charge you an interest rate that will compensate them for that moderate risk plus enough to make a profit. That means that you have to reinvest that money in an investment that will pay you a higher rate of interest and is also very safe. That usually is not possible. I realize that there are sometimes tax advantages in this technique, but I don't believe they are worth the risk. Remember that retirement is not the time of your life when you want to lose sleep over your investments.

LIFE INSURANCE

Most people purchase life insurance to provide for the welfare and income of surviving family in case they die prematurely. For the retired person, these needs are smaller and that's why most reduce or eliminate life insurance after their working years. Before making a decision about life insurance, it is important to understand the differences between the two main types—term and whole or ordinary life.

Term Insurance. Term insurance gets its name from the fact that it provides protection for a specified term. In the case of term insurance, you pay a specified premium depending on age and health to a life insurance company. In return, they will agree that if you die within the term of the policy, they will pay a specified face amount of the policy to your beneficiary. At the end of the term for which you have paid the premium, the contract no longer exists and has no residual value to it. Usually, term insurance can be renewed by paying another premium. Naturally, for the older person, the premiums for this type of insurance are high because the risk of death is higher than for a younger person. If you choose to renew your policy at the end of the term, the premium usually goes up as your age goes up.

Whole or Ordinary Life. Ordinary life insurance is really a combination of term insurance and a savings plan. Unlike term insurance where the amount of the premium increases periodically, the premium on ordinary life stays constant year after year. The premiums for ordinary life insurance are often many times greater than that of term insurance. Part of each premium payment is set aside in the plan as a savings program on which the life insurance company will pay you interest. As long as you do not surrender the policy, the interest in the insurance policy accumulates tax-free.

Ordinary life insurance does provide permanent protection as long as the premiums are paid. The savings plan, however, is really not very competitive because the interest rates paid by the insurance companies are not as high as are available in other types of investments. In addition, the commissions paid to the life insurance agents are typically quite high on this type of insurance. Another type of ordinary life insurance is single premium whole life. This is normally purchased as an investment and will be covered in the investment section.

Universal Life. As interest rates began to climb in the late 70s and early 80s, the insurance companies needed a product to retain their policy holders. That product became universal life. It is designed much like ordinary life insurance in that it is a combination of term insurance and a savings plan. The interest rates paid on universal life policies are similar to those offered in money market funds. This combination of higher interest rates plus the benefits of tax-free accumulation has offered a good alternative to the younger investor who is trying to accumulate assets.

Swapping Policies. As noted in the discussion on universal life, the life insurance industry has become very competitive over the last few years. Prior to that, the policies that they issued paid very low interest rates, normally 3 or 4 percent. By taking the time to investigate your old insurance policies, you may find some hidden value. Many people have accumulated life insurance policies that are fully paid up or in which they are only earning 3 or 4 percent. Assuming that they still need the insurance protection, those policies can be swapped for more updated ones that pay higher current interest rates. In addition, those policies normally have borrowing provisions allowing you to borrow out the money at very low interest rates, normally around 5 percent. It is possible to borrow the value of those life insurance policies and reinvest the proceeds in investments that offer higher current return.

The Need for Insurance. Normally insurance is used to protect the family against the premature loss of the breadwinner. As you enter into your retirement years, the need for life insurance is dramatically reduced. Many people continue making large premium payments on policies bought years before without thinking through the need for life insurance. By updating older policies and eliminating those that are not necessary, you can save substantial sums that can be reinvested more productively. An insurance worksheet is provided in the Appendix.

One need for life insurance that should be considered is that of estate planning. If you are not the owner of a life insurance policy and if the death proceeds of life insurance are payable to a specified beneficiary, there are no estate taxes. In addition, you may consider life insurance if your estate has assets that are not easily convertible into cash. In this case, the life insurance proceeds can be used by the estate for the purpose of paying estate taxes, administrative costs and providing for the beneficiary while the other assets are being liquidated.

SUMMARY

1. Do your planning together as husband and wife; the experience can be rewarding.
2. Establish a budget to determine exactly what income will be necessary to achieve the life-style you desire.
3. Determine your sources of income: the amount of social security, your pension, and how much you will need from your investments.
4. Evaluate the investments that you already have to see if they are proper for your new retirement situation.

CHAPTER FOUR

Predicting the Future

In this chapter you will learn how to determine what your future income and expenses will be based on your assumption about inflation. By anticipating the future, you can make adjustments now if your income will not be enough to meet your expenses.

If pressed, I would have to admit that exact investment results cannot be predicted. That's why diversification is so important. Maybe a better title for this chapter would be preparing for the future. Preparing in the sense that you must anticipate how much your living expenses are going to be 5, 10, 15, or even 20 years from now. By doing so, you will be able to determine exactly how much income you will need from your investments to meet these expenses. Once that has been determined, you will then be better able to select the investments that will provide the necessary income.

You may already be retired and, therefore, already have a good estimate of your living expenses. If you have not yet retired, it's important that you begin making some estimates of what you will need. If you completed the worksheet from Chapter 3, you will have already established your budget. Be sure to separate your expenses into fixed expenses and variable expenses.

FIXED OR VARIABLE EXPENSES

Fixed expenses are those that are not expected to increase with inflation. Those expenses would be such items as home mortgage payments and payments on insurance policies. Variable expenses, on the other hand, are expenses that would be expected to increase with inflation. Most of your expenses will fall into this category, such as food, utilities, automobile expenses, and entertainment. For the purpose of predicting the amount of income you will need 10 years from now, it's extremely important to make a fairly accurate distinction between the two types of expenses. Remember Bill and Susan Retiree? They had no house payment or any other fixed expenses. All of their expenses totaling $19,350 were variable expenses and could be expected to increase with inflation.

In order to predict the amount of your future expenses, you must make an assumption of what the inflation rate will be. I know that is extremely difficult to predict, but you have to make at least an educated guess. Assuming an inflation rate of between 5 and 7 percent over the next 10 years seems reasonable.

Now that you have estimated your cost of living if you were retired today, it's time to find out how much money you are going to need in the future. It's really quite simple with the aid of Table 4–1 and a little multiplication.

Along the top of Table 4–1 are several inflation rates: 3, 5, 7, and 10 percent. Going down the left side are various periods in the future: 5, 10, 15, and 20 years. This table is used to anticipate the increase in your variable expenses based on your assumption of what the inflation rate will be in the future.

How does it work? If you want to find out how much your variable expenses will be in 10 years based on a 7 percent inflation factor, simply multiply the amount of your current variable expenses by the factor 1.97. This will give you the approximate dollar amount of your variable expenses in 10 years. Let's use Bill and Susan as an example.

Table 4–2 is the budget established by Bill and Susan Retiree. As you remember, they had no fixed expenses and $19,350 in variable expenses. To find out how much their

TABLE 4–1
Inflation Factors for Variable Expenses
and Social Security or Pension Income

	3 Percent	5 Percent	7 Percent	10 Percent
5 years	1.16	1.28	1.40	1.60
10 years	1.34	1.63	1.97	2.59
15 years	1.56	2.08	2.76	4.18
20 years	1.81	2.56	3.87	6.73

expenses will be in 10 years, assuming a 7 percent inflation rate, simply multiply $19,350 by 1.97 and you will find that their variable expenses will be $38,119. To find out how much their total expenses would be, you would add $38,119 to their current fixed expenses. Remember, fixed expenses are not anticipated to increase with inflation, so you use the same amount you are currently spending. In Bill and Susan's case, they have no fixed expenses, so their total expenses in 10 years should approximate $38,119. That's right; in 10 years, they can expect their expenses will double. That is one sharp side of the two-edged sword of inflation.

PROJECTING YOUR FUTURE INCOME

Now that you know how much it's going to cost you to live, let's see if you can afford it. Your next major step is to evaluate what your income is going to be in the future. This is no more difficult than approximating your expenses. There are four primary sources of income: pension plans, social security, income derived from fixed-income investments, and income derived from growth-oriented investments. Each of these four sources of income must be evaluated separately.

Bill and Susan Retiree have all four sources of income, so let's use them as an example again. Start with the pension income. In recent years, some pension plans have made provisions for automatic cost-of-living increases. Some plans will increase your benefits by 1 percent for every 1 percent increase in the inflation rate. Other plans may increase your benefit by one half of the inflation rate. Most plans, however,

TABLE 4-2
Current Income and Expenses for
Bill and Susan Retiree

	Amount	Rate	Income
Earned income			$ 0
Pension			4,910
Social security			9,864
Growth income	$ 8,700	5.60%	487
Fixed income	127,600	8.78	11,200
	$136,300	8.57%	$26,461
Fixed expenses			
House payment	$ 0		
Total fixed expenses	$ 0		
Variable expenses			
Utilities	$ 1,800		
Food	3,500		
Clothing	1,000		
Income taxes	1,850		
Property taxes	800		
Transportation	2,100		
Medical	1,000		
Debt repayment	0		
Maintenance	500		
Insurance	900		
Vacations	2,400		
Contributions	1,000		
Gifts	1,000		
Furnishings	500		
Other	1,000		
Other	0		
Total variable expenses	$ 19,350		
Total expenses	$ 19,350		
Savings	$ 7,111		

do not have automatic cost-of-living adjustments. It is important for you to find out what your pension benefit is and if it has cost-of-living adjustments. Bill Retiree's pension benefit of $4,910 a year does not have cost-of-living adjustments. That means in future years he will continue to receive a constant $4,910 per year no matter what the inflation rate is.

Social security is probably the most difficult of all the four income sources to evaluate. The reason is obvious; increases are at the whim of Congress. In doing evaluations for clients, I take the middle-of-the-road approach. If I'm assuming that inflation will be 6 percent, I further assume that social security benefits will be raised by half of the inflation rate or 3 percent. Since we used a 7 percent inflation factor in determining how much Bill and Susan's expenses will be in 10 years, let's use approximately half of that or a 3 percent inflation factor to find out how much their social security will be in 10 years. To determine that, simply go to the 3 percent column on Table 4–1, and you will find a new inflation factor of 1.34. Now, multiply the amount they are currently receiving in social security ($9,864) by 1.34 and you will find that they will be receiving $13,217 10 years from now.

Determining how much they will receive from the fixed income portion of their portfolio is the easiest of all. By definition, the return from fixed-income investments will not increase in future years no matter what inflation is. Therefore, you can anticipate that you will be receiving the same amount of income 10 years from now as you receive now. In the case of Bill and Susan, they are currently receiving $11,200 from fixed-income investments.

To determine the amount that you will be receiving in growth asset income 10 years from now, use Table 4–3. This table is used only to determine the future amounts of growth asset income. Why is that? Won't the growth assets grow at the same rate as inflation? Remember the Goldman Sachs study from Chapter 2? When you take an average of the growth rate of common stocks and real estate, you find that they grew approximately 37 percent faster than the rate of inflation. Therefore, if inflation is 10 percent per year, you can expect growth assets to increase in value at 13.7 percent per year. Therefore, Table 4–3 reflects that additional growth.

Bill and Susan had a small amount invested in a common stock mutual fund. They are receiving $487 from that fund. To determine how much they will receive 10 years in the future at 7 percent inflation rate, simply multiply $487 by 2.69. Ten years from now, we can anticipate that they will be receiving $1,310 in growth income.

TABLE 4–3
Inflation Factors for Growth Income

	3 Percent	5 Percent	7 Percent	10 Percent
5 years	1.59	1.75	1.92	2.21
10 years	1.84	2.23	2.69	3.55
15 years	2.13	2.85	3.78	5.72
20 years	2.47	3.64	5.30	9.22

PUTTING IT ALL TOGETHER

Now let's put this all together using Bill and Susan again. Table 4–4 sums up Bill and Susan's income and expense projections. You may use this example to project your own future income and expenses.

TABLE 4–4

Current variable expenses of $19,350 × 1.97	= $38,119
Current fixed expenses of $0 × N/A	= _____0
Total projected expenses	$38,119
Current pension benefit of $4,910 × Fixed	= $ 4,910
Current social security of $9,864 × 1.34	= 13,217
Current fixed income of $11,200 × Fixed	= 11,200
Current growth income of $487 × 2.69	= _1,310
Total projected income	$30,637

As you can see, Bill and Susan have a bit of a problem. Their expenses now exceed their income. Tables 4–5, 4–6, and 4–7 illustrate a 25-year projection of income and expenses for Bill and Susan assuming 5 percent, 7 percent, and 10 percent inflation. The numbers vary slightly from our previous example due to rounding.

What do Bill and Susan do now? They can start to spend their principal, they can cut back on their life-style, they can start to sweat, or they can keep reading to find out how they

TABLE 4–5
Current Situation
(inflation rate assumption of 5 percent)

Year	Income	Expenses	Savings
1985	$26,461	$19,350	$ 7,111
1986	26,706	20,318	6,389
1987	26,958	21,333	5,624
1988	27,216	22,400	4,816
1989	27,482	23,520	3,962
1990	27,756	24,696	3,060
1991	28,037	25,931	2,107
1992	28,327	27,227	1,100
1993	28,625	28,589	37
1994	28,932	30,018	(1,086)
1995	29,249	31,519	(2,270)
1996	29,575	33,095	(3,520)
1997	29,911	34,750	(4,839)
1998	30,257	36,487	(6,230)
1999	30,615	38,312	(7,697)
2000	30,984	40,227	(9,244)
2001	31,364	42,239	(10,874)
2002	31,757	44,351	(12,593)
2003	32,163	46,568	(14,405)
2004	32,583	48,896	(16,313)
2005	33,017	51,341	(18,324)
2006	33,465	53,908	(20,443)
2007	33,929	56,604	(22,674)
2008	34,410	59,434	(25,024)
2009	34,907	62,406	(27,498)

might better invest their assets so they can continue to enjoy the life-style they currently have. The next chapter will illustrate the attributes of the perfect investment. We will again use Bill and Susan Retiree to determine what specific investment benefits they need in order to maintain their life-style in retirement.

TABLE 4–6
Current Situation
(inflation rate assumption of 7 percent)

Year	Income	Expenses	Savings
1985	$26,461	$19,350	$ 7,111
1986	26,804	20,705	6,100
1987	27,160	22,154	5,006
1988	27,530	23,705	3,826
1989	27,915	25,364	2,551
1990	28,315	27,139	1,176
1991	28,732	29,039	(307)
1992	29,167	31,072	(1,905)
1993	29,619	33,247	(3,628)
1994	30,091	35,574	(5,483)
1995	30,584	38,064	(7,480)
1996	31,098	40,729	(9,631)
1997	31,636	43,580	(11,944)
1998	32,198	46,631	(14,432)
1999	32,786	49,895	(17,708)
2000	33,402	53,387	(19,985)
2001	34,048	57,124	(23,077)
2002	34,725	61,123	(26,398)
2003	35,436	65,402	(29,966)
2004	36,182	69,980	(33,797)
2005	36,967	74,878	(37,911)
2006	37,794	80,120	(42,326)
2007	38,664	85,728	(47,064)
2008	39,581	91,729	(52,148)
2009	40,549	98,150	(57,601)

TABLE 4–7
Current Situation
(inflation rate assumption of 10 percent)

Year	Income	Expenses	Savings
1985	$26,461	$ 19,350	$ 7,111
1986	26,951	21,285	5,666
1987	27,468	23,414	4,054
1988	28,014	25,755	2,259
1989	28,591	28,330	261
1990	29,203	31,163	(1,961)
1991	29,851	34,280	(4,429)
1992	30,539	37,708	(7,169)
1993	31,270	41,478	(10,208)
1994	32,048	45,626	(13,578)
1995	32,877	50,189	(17,312)
1996	33,761	55,208	(21,447)
1997	34,706	60,729	(26,023)
1998	35,717	66,801	(31,085)
1999	36,800	73,482	(36,681)
2000	37,964	80,830	(42,866)
2001	39,215	88,913	(46,698)
2002	40,563	97,804	(57,241)
2003	42,018	107,584	(65,566)
2004	43,591	118,343	(74,752)
2005	45,295	130,177	(84,883)
2006	47,143	143,195	(96,051)
2007	49,153	157,514	(108,361)
2008	51,342	173,266	(121,923)
2009	53,731	190,592	(136,861)

SUMMARY

1. Variable expenses will increase with inflation, fixed expenses will not.
2. Growth income will increase with inflation, fixed income will not.
3. In projecting future social security benefits, assume they will be increased at one half the inflation rate.
4. Six percent inflation is a reasonable inflation assumption over the next decade.

The Perfect Investment

If you were given the opportunity to construct the perfect investment, what benefits would it have? You would probably want it to be very safe. You would want it to have high liquidity. It should provide a high level of income but, at the same time, give you some growth opportunities. In addition, you would want to keep the IRS away so tax advantages would be important. There may be some other additional benefits you might add; but safety, liquidity, high income, growth potential, and tax advantages make up the five major investment benefits. Let's define each of these benefits.

Safety. This is the most important investment benefit to the retiree. Safety involves the guarantee that none of your principal will ever be lost. Safety, in a broader sense, means that none of the purchasing power of your principal will ever be lost.

Liquidity. Liquidity is a term that you all should know. The concept is very simple. If the investment you make allows you to withdraw your money when you wish, quickly, easily, and without penalty, then it would be considered liquid.

Retired persons should keep at least three to six months' income in short-term, liquid investments such as money market funds. It is important that you have easily accessible cash in case of some emergency. The remainder of your investment funds should be put into longer-term investments that offer a higher rate of return. With good planning, you can have the best of both worlds; enough liquidity to meet emergencies and most of your investments in longer-term commitments that allow you to maximize your investment earnings. Remember your goal. You want to get your money working as hard as possible so that *you* don't have to.

Income.   Now that you are retired, you will want your investments to pay you a cash income periodically, perhaps every month or every quarter. Investments in which you make a loan usually offer consistent current income as their major benefit. These include such things as bonds, certificates of deposit, unit investment trust, and the like. Many of these fixed-income investments are well suited for retirees.

Growth.   The term *growth investments* has become synonymous with common stocks and real estate. In most cases, the primary benefit of these investments is to offer you appreciation. They are usually purchased with the intent that they will be held for a period of time and then sold at a value greater than their purchase price. They may also provide current income during the time that they are held. It is important that retirees have some growth assets in their investment portfolio. As we discussed in Chapter 2, growth investments are usually those in which you own the asset.

Tax Benefits.   Many retirees of seemingly moderate income find themselves in high tax brackets. There are several reasons for these high rates. Many have paid off the mortgage on their houses and, therefore, have no interest deductions. In addition, their children have moved away, so they get no deductions from those dependents. For investors in higher tax brackets, searching out investments that have tax benefits can provide a significant advantage. There are a number of very high-quality growth and income investments that offer significant tax advantages. For growth investments, the primary tax advantage is that of long-term capital gains. Under the current tax law, if you hold an asset like a common stock or real estate for longer than six months, only 40 percent of the amount of the gain is taxable upon sale. The other 60 percent of the gain is received tax-free.[1]

Income-oriented investments, such as municipal bonds and some life insurance policies, receive very favorable tax treatment. In the case of municipal bonds, the income received is not subject to federal income taxes. Under current tax legislation, some insurance policies also offer an excellent method of receiving high, current, tax-free income in a very safe investment.

NO SECRET FORMULA

Safety, liquidity, income, growth, and tax advantages are the five benefits of the perfect investment. Unfortunately, there is no perfect investment. Each investment does some things very well but is weak in others. Money market funds, as an example, are very safe, extremely liquid, but their rates of return are average and they have no growth opportunities or tax advantages. Real estate, on the other hand, has good growth potential and some tax advantages, but it is not very liquid and usually does not pay high income. The problem is that you probably need some of each of the investment benefits and no single investment can provide that.

Look at your own situation as an example. You may have a need for safety of principal but, at the same time, you need a hedge against inflation. You may need some liquidity in your investments, but you also want the highest investment return possible. That's okay. All these seemingly conflicting objectives can be achieved at the same time. Remember, you are not looking for the one perfect investment. There is no such thing. Rather, you should look for the right combination of investments to meet your own investment objectives. Remember also, when making investments, you should not just be concerned about the dollars that you can earn but also about your own peace of mind. No investment, no matter how high the potential return, is worth losing sleep over.

---

[1] The U.S. Congress was debating capital gains treatment as this book went to press.

THE RIGHT STUFF

Many of you have had high school or college chemistry. One morning in my high school chemistry class, the teacher walked in and put two beakers of clear liquid on the desk in front of him. He held up the first beaker and explained it was a very strong acid solution. He proceeded to drop in a piece of aluminum and it immediately dissolved. He held up the second beaker and explained that it was a very strong basic solution. He then dropped another piece of material into that solution and it bubbled and foamed for a minute and then disappeared. Obviously, either one of these solutions would have eaten the flesh right off his hand. He then proceeded to empty the contents of both beakers and to combine them together in a third larger beaker. He held it up in front of the class, swirled it around, and then drank it. I have to admit, I felt two strong emotions at the time. The first was concern for my chemistry teacher. The second emotion, while I hate to admit it, was excitement about the possibility of that being the last chemistry class I would ever have to attend! Unfortunately, however, there I was the next day, in the same chemistry class with the same chemistry teacher.

Those of you who have had some chemistry background will realize that by mixing the strong acid and the strong base, the solutions neutralize each other and actually become a useful, harmless substance. The same can be true with investments. If you have too much of your money invested in one area, it can be damaging to your overall portfolio. By having the proper mix of investments, you can enjoy a much higher overall rate of return without taking undue risk.

WHY SOME INVESTORS DO WELL

Why do some investors seem to do so well while others earn only a mediocre return on their investments? The investor who gets the higher return has chosen the right combination of investments.

Some investments have more risk and offer higher returns. Some allow you to get your money at a moment's notice and others are less liquid and involve a long-term commitment. Some offer tax benefits and others offer high income. If you want an investment that offers high liquidity, you are going to have to accept a lower rate of return. A case in point is a passbook savings account versus a long-term certificate of deposit. If you give a banker your money and tell him that you want to have the privilege of taking it out every day, he can offer you a passbook account. However, if you go to the same banker and tell him that you will give them your money for a year, he will pay you a much higher rate. You now have a choice. You can have an investment with immediate access to your money but with a low return or one with a much higher rate of return and sacrifice some liquidity. By planning properly, you will be able to get the best of both worlds. As an example, you might invest a portion of your funds in a short-term passbook account to provide quick access in case of an emergency. That will allow you to invest most of your funds in long-term investments that pay higher yields. You won't have to worry about taking out your long-term investment early to meet an emergency because that is the purpose of the passbook account. The key to successful investing is proper diversification.

DIVERSIFICATION

The dictionary defines diversity as "to make diverse, give variety to, vary." When used in a business context, diversity is defined as "to distribute (investments) among several companies in order to average the risk of loss." Diversification may be one of the most important concepts in investing. Most people think of it as owning several different stocks instead of just one. That's one application, but the concept is broader than that. It really means owning a variety of investments rather than just one. As you plan your investment strategy, don't just think of the individual investments by themselves. Think of how they will work in combination with your other investments to achieve your desired goals.

DIVERSIFICATION LOWERS RISK

One of the most important reasons to diversify is to lower your risk. If you were to put all your eggs in one basket, buy one high-growth common stock as an example, you might have a chance of hitting the jackpot. On the other hand, the company could go bankrupt and you could lose your entire investment. No matter how good an investment opportunity sounds, never allow it to become a disproportionately large part of your investment holdings. There are too many unpredictable events that cause the best laid plans not to work out.

General Public Utilities looked like an excellent long-term, safe investment. The electric utility provided electrical power for a stable area of the country and the stock paid a generous dividend. You may not recognize the name General Public Utilities, but you will recognize the name Three Mile Island. The common stock of this utility company had provided a good return for its investors until the nuclear accident at Three Mile Island. Following that unpredictable, unforeseen event, the price of the stock plummeted overnight and the dividend was eliminated.

How about Washington Public Power Supply tax-free municipal bonds? It seemed like a great concept. Build a large nuclear power generating plant in the growing Northwest. All the utilities in the area would buy power from the plant; they would even sign contracts requiring them to pay for the power generated even if they didn't use it. Investors purchased billions of dollars of tax-free municipal bonds to pay for the construction of the generating plant. After all, the concept was sound. The bonds were rated Triple A by a major rating service and the high tax-free return was very attractive. Now, several years later, the lower demand for electrical power, the high cost of overruns caused by inflation, and some questionable court decisions that let many utilities off the hook have cost many investors billions of savings dollars. In some cases, investors lost most of their life's savings.

No investor could be faulted for making an investment in either Washington Public Power or General Public Utilities. The events that caused their decline could not have been predicted. The mistake would have been to place too great a percentage of money in either of these two investments. Diversification will reduce your risk and help provide you with good consistent investment returns.

AVOID VOLATILE INVESTMENTS

Diversification can offer another advantage too. It reduces the volatility of your overall investments. Many of you have experienced the exciting feeling of reading the morning paper to discover that your stock has gone up two points. It makes for a terrific day. Many, too, have experienced the sinking feeling of finding out that your stock went down. Investments that are too volatile can be nerve-racking. Retirement should be free of this kind of stress.

Having investments that are volatile may also contribute to some poor investment decisions. In 1979, many investors in common stocks were disappointed as stock prices remained low. On the other hand, those who had invested their money in real estate watched their properties appreciate at sometimes 2 percent per month. Many investors who had all their growth investments in common stocks felt compelled to sell their stock at very low prices and reinvest in already inflated real estate. Just three years later, in 1982, real estate prices leveled off and the stock market went into one of the greatest rallies in history. No one has the ability, intuition, or foresight to consistently be invested in just the right place. The lesson is to be diversified. If half of your growth investment portfolio were in common stocks and the other half in real estate in 1979, you may have been disappointed in the performance of your stock market investments but would have been cheered by what was happening to your real estate holdings. Your overall investment would have been providing consistent, positive results. Fear that the stock market was going to continue down or that real estate was going to continue up forever would not have influenced you into a bad investment decision.

HOW TO DIVERSIFY

What mixture of investments is exactly right for you? Naturally, I cannot answer that precisely because I don't know you personally. The proper investment mix depends upon your needs, your financial circumstances, and your psychological tolerance for different kinds of investments. Recognizing that I lack specific information about you, let me give you some general parameters for investment.

1. You should keep enough liquidity in a bank passbook account or money market fund to equal between three and six months' income.

2. The growth portion of your investment portfolio should range between 20 percent and 50 percent of your total portfolio. The growth investment should be equally divided between real estate and common stocks. You will normally want these growth investments to provide you with some current income also.

3. The remainder of your investments should be in high-quality, fixed, income-oriented assets of intermediate to long-term maturities. Approximately one half of your fixed income investment should be in such things as long-term municipal, corporate, or government bonds. These yield high income but you do take some risk of principal fluctuation during the holding period. The other half of your fixed income investments should be placed in things such as CDs, annuities, or life insurance investments where you have no risk of principal variation.

4. Investments that offer tax benefits usually have lower yields than those that don't. The tax benefits compensate for the lower yield if you are in a high enough tax bracket. If you are in a tax bracket of 25 percent or above, it is usually advantageous to be invested where you receive tax-free yields. Municipal bonds and some life insurance investments offer attractive tax-free income. The return received in some real estate investments as well as a portion of the dividends on some utility common stocks can also be received without having to pay current federal income taxes.

Naturally, the exact selection of an investment portfolio should be tailored specifically to your needs. It depends on your investment temperament and your specific investment objectives. If your portfolio of investments is substantial, there may be some beneficial estate tax ramifications to certain kinds of investments. You should consult an estate tax attorney if you are in that situation.

SUMMARY

1. Unless you truly enjoy the action, avoid volatile investments.
2. Diversify—never have too much of your money invested in one area no matter how good it sounds.
3. Keep from three to six months' income in liquid investments like savings accounts or money markets.
4. For most retirees, between 20 percent and 50 percent of your money should be invested to provide for growth.
5. Keep at least 50 percent of your assets in high-yielding, fixed-income investments.

_____

CHAPTER SIX

The Thrill of Victory and the Agony of Defeat

"What a beautiful day, perfect for golf," Charles thought as he opened the paper to the financial section. "Appleplex 17, down two points!" he gasped, reaching for the phone.

"I'm sorry, Mr. Smith, your broker is not in just yet."

"Typical," Charles thought, "I will call him after my golf game." Visions of Appleplex down again flashed through his mind as his tee shot bounced helplessly off to the right and into the pond. A 49; that's the worst nine hole score since he retired.

While the rest of the foursome were resting, he called his broker. "I'm sorry, Mr. Smith, he's just left for lunch, but he does need to talk to you. Something about Appleplex and bad earnings; I'm not sure exactly what the specifics are."

Mercifully, the last putt fell into the cup. "What did you have, Charles?" asked one of his buddies. "Nine for the hole, 113 for the round," he remarked curtly as he headed for his car.

"How was your game, dear?" his wife asked.

"Terrible! I've got to make a call," he answered.

"I'm sorry, Mr. Smith, he's just left for the day. He said to tell you that Appleplex was down five points but not to worry, he would talk to you tomorrow."

Those who like the thrill of victory and the agony of defeat may choose to be involved in investments that require day-to-day monitoring. Unless you really enjoy being part of the process, you should make long-term investment decisions and leave the day-to-day monitoring to the professionals.

TWO WAYS TO INVEST

There are two ways to participate in most investments: do it yourself or let the professionals do it. Unless you enjoy the process of investing and are especially good at it, you should try to select passive investments that don't involve day-to-day investment decisions. These more passive investments will probably produce a more consistent return and make your life more enjoyable too. What kind of investments are we talking about?

THREE TYPES OF PASSIVE INVESTMENTS

There are three major types of passive or managed investments; mutual funds, unit trusts, and limited partnerships. The one that you select depends on the type of benefits that suit your investment needs. If you need growth assets like common stocks in your portfolio, mutual funds are usually your best choice. If you are looking for fixed-income investments such as municipal, corporate, or government bonds, unit investment trusts will suit your purpose. Your best bet for investing in real estate is through a real estate limited partnership.

MUTUAL FUNDS

The concept of the mutual fund is simple. The money of a large number of investors is pooled together and invested by a professional money manager. The type of investments they make depends on the objective for that particular mutual fund. If the objective is for rapid growth, the mutual fund manager may select only growth-oriented common stocks. On the other hand, if the objective is high current income and moderate growth, an investment in common stocks of more mature companies who pay higher dividends would be appropriate.

Mutual funds are not restricted just to investments in common stocks. Some funds may only invest in bonds. The function of the fund manager is to watch the investments in the fund to be sure they are performing as they should. If some are not, they will be sold and replaced by others.

Besides the convenience of having professional money managers select and watch over your investments, mutual funds offer another distinct advantage: diversification. Most investors have limited capital and therefore are not able to purchase a diversified portfolio. By pooling your money with other investors, you create a pool of funds that is large enough to invest in a large number of issues.

When you buy a share in a mutual fund, you own a proportionate interest in the total portfolio of the fund. Some mutual funds will allow you to invest as little as $25 at a time. There is no other practical way with $25 or with $25,000 that you could get a truly diversified portfolio. Mutual funds are available in two major types: closed end and open end.

Closed End Mutual Funds

A closed end fund will accept a specific amount of money from investors and then not take any more. Once this specific offering period is over, the fund is considered closed to any new investors. After the fund is closed, the shares can be bought or sold in the over-the-counter market or on one of the listed exchanges. If an investor wants to buy shares in a closed end fund after the initial offering period, he can buy them through his stockbroker from a shareholder who wants to sell. Conversely, if an investor in a closed end fund would like to sell, he simply sells his shares to somebody else through his stockbroker. The amount an investor receives when he sells his shares may or may not bear a direct relationship to the net asset value. Like other common stocks traded in the open market, the price of this security depends upon the supply and demand (the number of investors who want to buy and the number of investors who want to sell). Depending on a number of factors, the investor may receive more or less than the net asset value. Because the shares of these funds are traded on the exchange, when you buy or sell shares you pay a regular commission to your stockbroker.

Open End Mutual Funds

A mutual fund is considered open end if, from time to time (some offer it continually), the fund will accept new money from investors. The new money that is taken into the pool is simply added to what is there and new investments are made. A new investor has no effect on the other investors in the pool. The price the new investor pays for the new shares of the fund is equal to the "net asset value" per share of the fund plus a commission if there is one. The "net asset value" is the value of all of the assets of the fund divided by the total number of shares. Every day, the open end mutual fund determines the value of the assets in the fund and calculates the net asset value per share at the end of the day. An investor desiring to liquidate would sell his shares back to the fund for the net asset value. Open end funds are divided into two additional categories: load and no-load.

Load or No-Load Mutual Funds

Load funds are those where a commission is paid to a salesperson to market it. The commissions can range up to 8½ percent of the amount of money invested. No-load funds do not have a commission. Most investment books written recently will tell you to invest in no-load mutual funds. Why not? It would seem to make good sense to avoid paying a commission.

That kind of advice is too simplistic. Unfortunately, most of these books are written by professional authors, not by people with extensive investment experience.

Using the same logic, it would make sense to shop around for the cheapest surgeon to do your bypass heart surgery. Obviously, that's not what you would do. You would not shop for the cheapest surgeon because the results of the operation are so important. As a matter of fact, you may look for the one that's the most expensive figuring that you get what you pay for.

The most important criteria for selecting a mutual fund are its objectives. They must fit your individual investment needs. The second most important is the long-term track record of the fund. Do they have consistent long-term performance?

Why do some mutual funds pay commissions to salespeople and others don't? It's simply a marketing decision. The management of load funds feel that the most effective method of attracting new buyers is to pay a commission to a financial planner or stockbroker. So, how do no-load funds attract new business? Just open up *The Wall Street Journal* and you will see advertisements for no-load mutual funds. You will find them in *Forbes, Business Week, Fortune, Money,* and other business magazines. Where does the money come from for all that advertising? You guessed it, in higher fees charged by the no-load mutual fund management. Once again, we learn "There ain't no free lunch." No-load may mean no visible load.

The important question is, "What do you get for the commission that you pay?" If you feel you have the time, energy, and expertise to select and monitor the proper mutual fund for your investment needs, then you should consider a no-load mutual fund. If you do seek investment advice from a stockbroker or a financial planner, the payment of the commission can be dollars very well spent.

Remember, be sure the objectives of the fund meet your investment needs and look for funds with a long-term consistent rate of return. You should look for 10 years of performance to ensure consistent results.

One final note on mutual funds. Often, new mutual funds are created for the purpose of investing in some specialized area. It may be a fund to invest in just high technology stocks, in gold stocks, or in health care stocks. Stay away from those funds when they are newly issued. Normally, those funds are brought to market when that particular kind of investment is very popular. When an investment is extremely popular and everybody is buying it, it is usually the wrong time to invest.

UNIT TRUSTS

A unit trust is very much like the mutual fund. A number of investors pool their resources to purchase a diversified portfolio of a particular kind of investment. Unit trusts are normally used to invest in fixed-income securities like corporate bonds, municipal bonds, and government bonds. The primary difference between the unit trust and a mutual fund is that once the unit trust investment portfolio has been selected, it is usually not changed.

Suppose a unit trust had as its objective, the purchase of municipal bonds (safe tax-free income). The unit trust manager would assemble a diversified portfolio of municipal bonds totaling $10 million, consisting of 15 to 20 different bond issues. This portfolio of bonds is then offered to investors in $1,000 increments. In buying a unit of the trust, an investor would purchase a proportionate share of the entire municipal bond portfolio. Once the bond portfolio has been established, it is not changed. Normally, the bonds are held until their maturity, at which time the proceeds from the maturing bonds are paid out to the unit trust holders.

Unit trusts are particularly attractive to investors who look for a consistent flow of income. Normally, a municipal, corporate, or government bond would pay its interest every six months. That is not very much help if you have monthly payments to make. The portfolio of bonds in the unit trust is arranged so that interest payments are coming in every month. The trust will determine the amount of the interest payments and then establish a consistent payment rate so you receive the same amount each month. The unit trust holder can elect to receive the interest every month, every quarter, or every six months. If you select the option every six months, you will get a slightly higher interest rate because the money remains invested slightly longer.

The safety involved in the unit trust is based on the quality of bonds in the portfolio. Naturally, if you have a unit trust comprised of government bonds, your safety is that of government bonds, AAA.

An investor needing to liquidate all or a portion of a unit trust holding can do so quite easily. The unit trust portfolio is evaluated every day and the unit holder is allowed to sell at the net asset value. The unit trust can offer one of the most effective methods of investing in government or municipal bonds.

There is a sales charge of about 4 percent on unit trusts. This is higher than the commission you might pay for purchasing individual bonds, but there is no sales charge to sell your unit trust investment like there would be with individual bonds. The sales charge is partially offset by the ability of the unit trust to purchase bonds in very large quantities. An investor buying half a million dollars worth of bonds is going to get a better price than someone buying $5,000 worth.

LIMITED PARTNERSHIPS

Another method of passive investing is through the limited partnership or syndication. While limited partnerships are not new, they have only recently become a popular form of investment. Unfortunately, many retired investors forgo the benefits of this type of investment because it's unfamiliar to them. There are several advantages with a limited partnership.

Passive Investment

Though it's called a limited partnership, there are actually two classes of partners: a general partner (there's usually one) and limited partners (of which there can be thousands). Generally speaking, it's the job of the general partner to provide the expertise in the investment and management of the real estate or other asset. The limited partners provide the investment capital. In explaining limited partnerships, I will use real estate as an example. However, this method of investing may be used with most other assets as well.

Pooling of Resources

The primary advantage of the limited partnership method is the ability to pool resources. By bringing hundreds or thousands of investors together, you can pool your investment dollars so that larger properties can be purchased. Often, by purchasing larger properties that most individual investors cannot afford, you can purchase at a lower cost per unit.

Public limited partnerships (those registered with the SEC) allow investors to participate with as little as a $5,000 investment. Each investor, or limited partner, is entitled to a proportionate share of the benefits based on the size of his or her investment. Often thousands of investors are attracted to a limited partnership syndication, providing the general partner with millions of dollars to invest.

The general partner will then take the proceeds and invest in various kinds of properties. Some syndications will invest in warehouses, shopping centers, apartment buildings, and office buildings all across the country. Others will specialize in one kind of property, while still others will specialize in one geographic area.

Expert Advice

If you have chosen your general partner properly, he or she is an expert in selecting real estate. It's his or her job to purchase the right property at the right price. It's also the general partner's job to manage those properties for you. He or she must be sure that the buildings stay leased, the payments for interest and taxes are made, and all other things that are necessary to operate the property are done. You, as a limited partner, truly become a passive investor. Periodically, as defined in the prospectus, you will receive a cash payment. Most partnerships do make quarterly cash payments to their limited partners.

Diversification

A great advantage of a limited partnership is diversification. Rather than having all your investment dollars in one property, it's normally spread among a number of properties. Diversification lowers your risk and helps ensure consistent results.

The general partner will begin selling the properties when he or she feels the time is right. When each property is sold and all expenses from the sale are paid, a proportionate share of the sales proceeds is paid to each limited partner. The general partner does not retain the sales proceeds for reinvestment. When the last property is sold and the last dollars are paid to the limited partners, the partnership is dissolved.

Limited Liability

Limited partners also have one other distinct advantage. As limited partners, they have limited liability. This simply means that under no circumstances (unless you have agreed to it) will you ever be required to put additional money into the partnership. If everything goes sour, you can only lose the amount that you have invested. The general partner, on the other hand, has general liability.

You may have guessed by now that general partners don't work for free. As a matter of fact, they can be very well paid. They normally collect a fee, usually in the form of a real estate commission, for investing the partnership money. They collect fees for the operation of the partnership, and they are normally entitled to some incentive compensation if profits work out according to projection. These fees are not necessarily bad. You would pay many of them yourself if you bought an individual rental property. The key is to get your money's worth. Most major real estate syndicators have pretty competitive fees. All the fees they charge are clearly spelled out in the prospectus.

You should be sure the fees are competitive, as well as check out the general partner to make sure he or she is experienced in the specific kind of real estate investment he or she is making. The prospectus offers you information about the previous track record of the general partner. If you are utilizing the services of a financial planner or stockbroker, he or she can help you select a program with a successful, well-regarded general partner.

PUBLIC AND PRIVATE PARTNERSHIPS

A public limited partnership is one registered with the SEC (Securities and Exchange Commission). In public partnerships, the syndicator normally wants to raise a large amount of money for the purchase of a diversified portfolio for real estate properties. In most syndications, the money is raised first and then the properties are purchased. This means that you really don't know what properties you are buying until after you have made your investment. That's not a major problem if you have a good general partner. The prospectus will tell you the kind of properties he or she anticipates purchasing.

Most real estate limited partnerships are private offerings. These offerings do not have to be registered with the SEC and normally involve no more than 35 partners. When you invest in a private offering, the property that is to be purchased is normally specified first. In this way, you know exactly what you are investing in. Private offerings can be very attractive if you find a good one. Many investors find comfort in knowing exactly what property they will be investing in. Be careful of private offerings because registration with the SEC is not required, and the area has some shady operators. It is more important than ever to check out the track record and the credentials of the general partner.

INVESTMENT ADVICE

Unless you are a very experienced investor, seek outside advice in planning your retirement portfolio. Where should you go to find such an advisor? Well, just like any other major decision, seek the counsel of friends and neighbors or others in similar situations as yourself. Interview your prospective advisor. It is very important that you have a clear line of communication and that you understand each other. It would be very helpful if he or she specialized in working with retired people.

Attorneys and CPAs may be experts in taxes and estate planning but are often not well informed about investments. Seek the advice of a financial planner or stockbroker who understands all aspects of investments. Deal with someone who is well known and well respected in the field. Remember, no one will be more concerned about your long-term welfare than you. Take the time to get informed about your various investment alternatives. Attend seminars, read books, do what is necessary to achieve a basic understanding of your various investment options. Above all, plan ahead.

Some retirees feel much more comfortable having their money managed on a full-time basis and without any of their own input. In this situation, the investor may delegate all the investment decisions to the money manager. Often, the investor does not know when changes are made or what investments are added or deleted from the portfolio. Where do you go to find such advice?

BANK TRUST DEPARTMENTS

Most major banking institutions have trust departments. These trust departments are set up with a specific goal of managing other people's assets. These trust departments, on the whole, do not have a good reputation for their advice. There may be reasons for their poor reputations. If your account with them is small (less than $1,000,000), you usually will not receive much personal service. In addition, the people working in managing money in bank trust departments are not typically well paid. The more competent money managers will soon leave the banking industry and establish themselves in the brokerage industry or as independents where they can make more money. This is not to say that all bank trust departments are inferior. If you choose to consider one, be sure to check it out thoroughly.

Why do many people use bank trust departments to manage their money? There is a presumption by many investors that because bank deposits are guaranteed by FDIC, the results of the trust department are also safe. A second reason is the stability of the banking institution itself. A husband wishing to take care of his wife after his death may leave their assets to be managed by a bank trust department. He does this knowing that the people at the bank may change but the bank will always be there. This can offer a sense of security to the surviving spouse. Unfortunately, the turnover in the bank trust department is very high. Therefore, the surviving spouse may be dealing with a number of different people as time goes on.

The cost of utilizing the bank trust department is not excessive. Generally they will charge between .8 percent to 1.5 percent of the value of the portfolio every year. In addition, there are some small additional transaction charges when money is processed in or out of the account.

INDEPENDENT MONEY MANAGERS

In almost every city there are independent money managers. These individuals are usually not associated with a bank or other financial institution. They are professionals whose job it is to manage the portfolios of others. Just as with the bank trust departments, there can be very good ones and others that are quite poor. Just as with a bank trust department, if you have a smaller account it does not receive much personal attention. The charge of independent money managers can range from as little as .5 percent to as much as 2 percent per year of value of the assets.

There are a number of pros and cons in working with stockbrokers, financial planners, bank trust departments, or independent money managers. The important thing is to select the method that is most suitable for you. If you don't mind giving up control of the selection of your investments, outside money management through a bank trust department or independent money manager may be appropriate. If you like to retain some control over your investments, which most people do, then going to a stockbroker or financial planner would be your best choice. No matter which you choose, be sure to openly share your needs and concerns. The individual assisting you in making financial decisions should be doing so with your best interests in mind. The planner can't be concerned about your interests until he or she knows exactly what your interests are.

SUMMARY

1. To better enjoy your retirement, make passive investments.

2. Mutual funds are a good way to invest in common stocks.
3. Unit trusts are a good way to invest in fixed-income securities.
4. Limited partnerships are a good way to invest in real estate.
5. Select an investment adviser whom you can communicate with.

Investing for Safety and Liquidity

In 1973, Merrill Lynch, the nation's largest stock brokerage firm, had a television advertisement offering investors 29 ways to invest in America. Today, there must be at least 129 ways.

Boy, what happened to the good old days, the simple days? All you had to do was invest your money in a passbook account or put it in a U.S. Series EE Bond and you knew you were doing the right thing.

In the last 10 years, there has been a revolution in financial services. Most of this has taken place because of deregulation. The revolution has provided an incredible number of opportunities for individual investors—so many that the choices can be bewildering and confusing. It can sometimes even be a little frightening.

Investors have become much more astute. They have to be. There are so many more choices, and those choices are much more complex. Many of the investment opportunities available today offer excellent potential returns for the individual investor. Today's investor who simply keeps money in the bank because that's what he or she has always done will miss a substantial investment opportunity.

The next three chapters won't cover 129 possible investment opportunities, but they will cover those investments that are appropriate for the retired investor. Many of the others available are too complicated or carry too much risk to be considered.

The discussion on specific investments is broken down into three major sections. Chapter 7 will cover investments whose primary benefit is liquidity, that is, the quick and easy access to your money. Chapter 8 will deal with long-term, fixed-income investments, those that pay you a stable consistent rate of income over a long period of time. Chapter 9 will cover growth investments such as common stocks and real estate.

The pros and cons of each of these basic investments will be covered. This will help you determine whether they are suitable for your situation. You will be able to compare how safe they are, how easily you can take your money out, and what kind of rate of return you might expect.

It won't be an in-depth study or explore every nook and cranny that only investment advisers need to know. But by the time you finish, you will have a pretty good idea of what benefits each investment offers and whether the investment is suitable for you.

To help summarize the investments and what benefits they provide, see Table 7–1.

SIX INVESTMENTS FOR SAFETY AND LIQUIDITY

At least some portion of your assets should be invested where you can access your money quickly and easily without penalty or risk. These highly liquid investments usually do not yield the highest rate of return. The higher-yielding investments usually involve some penalty or risk if you need to withdraw them early. By keeping some assets liquid, you have enough money to meet unforeseen emergencies with your liquid investments and can derive the higher yield benefits of longer-term investments with the remainder of your assets without the risk of liquidating them prior to maturity. There are six primary investments that are designed for liquidity: money market mutual funds, money market accounts, Treasury bills, savings accounts, certificates of deposit, and U.S. savings bonds.

TABLE 7–1

	Liquidity	Income	Growth	Safety of Principal	Tax Advantage
Savings account	H	L	N	H	N
CD	M	M	N	H	N
Money market	H	L	N	H	N
T-bill	H	L	N	H	L
Savings bond	M	L	N	H	N
Corporate bond	M	H	L	M	N
Government bond	M	H	L	M	N
GNMA	M	H	L	M	N
Municipal bond	M	H	L	M	H
Zero-coupon bond	M	N	L	M	N
Annuity	M	M	N	H	H
Single premium whole life insurance	H	M	N	H	H
Preferred stock	M	H	L	M	N
Common stock	M	M	H	M	M
Real estate	L	M	H	M	H

H = High
M = Medium
L = Low
N = None

MONEY MARKETS

In the middle 1970s, competition among the financial institutions brought one of the greatest deals to the American investor since compound interest: the money market fund and the money market account. The first to be offered were money market funds by the large stock brokerage firms. Money market funds allow many investors to pool their money for the purpose of investing in large certificates of deposit or other short-term securities such as commercial paper or Treasury bills. There were two major advantages: liquidity and competitive yield. Investors had instant access to their money and yet were paid interest rates well in excess of what was available in the normal passbook savings account. In just a few short years, over $250 billion had been invested by individuals in money market funds. So much money was taken out of banks for the purpose of depositing in money market funds that the banks needed a way to compete. The federal government lifted some restrictions and allowed banks to offer money market accounts.

Money Market Funds

The money market fund, the kind that was first established, is a mutual fund. When you deposit money in a money market fund, you actually become a shareholder. The money you invest along with that of other shareholders is invested in very high-quality, low-risk, short-term investments. As a shareholder, you receive whatever interest is paid on the investments made by the fund manager, less a small service fee for their bookkeeping and advice. Your money market fund is very safe because of the high-quality treasury bills, certificates of deposit, and commercial paper in which the fund manager invests.

Money Market Accounts

An investment in a bank money market account is just like any other deposit at that bank. The funds become a general asset of the bank and can be used to make any kind of loan or investment that the bank wishes. As long as the bank has FDIC insurance, your deposit up to $100,000 is insured by an agency of the federal government. The rate of interest you receive on your money market account is determined by the bank and posted every month. You will not receive the full amount that they receive on the loans that are made with your deposits. The bank will pay you the rate of interest they choose depending on how badly they want your money. When the bank money market accounts first became available, they were paying rates in excess of what were available in the money market funds. The banks did this to lure back the deposits that they had lost. Currently, bank money market accounts and money market funds pay about the same interest rate.

For all practical purposes, the safety of the money market

accounts at banks and the money market mutual funds is about the same. At banks you do have the FDIC insurance protection up to $100,000. This is not true with money market funds. However, the investments by the money market fund managers are in extremely safe and extremely high-quality, short-term commercial and government obligations. Billions of dollars have been attracted into both money market accounts and money market mutual funds, and no one has ever lost a dime.

One of the other main attractions of money markets is liquidity. In most cases, you can have access to your money by simply writing a check on your account. Some money markets allow you to access your money by telephone, and they will send you a check. Each money market has different restrictions on how you can access your money. Some allow unlimited check writing, others allow only three checks a month. In some cases, there are service charges for the checks that you write. Minimum deposits in the money markets can range from as little as $500 to as high as $10,000, depending on the institution. Money markets are very competitive and the rates offered are very close. Pick the one with features that best suit your needs.

Remember the story about there being no free lunch? Well, the same is true with money markets. You do have great liquidity and you have a competitive yield. But, you also take the interest rate risk that is normally taken by the bank or other financial institutions. What is "interest rate risk"? The interest rate that you receive on your money market can change every day. If economic conditions are such that the interest rates are dropping, you will be receiving less interest each day on your deposit. Conversely, if interest rates are rising, you will receive a higher interest rate each day. Because of this, the risk of changing interest rates is now yours. That can work to your advantage or your disadvantage. Obviously, if interest rates are rising, you don't want to have your money locked into a long-term bond or long-term certificate of deposit. It would be better placed in a money market where the interest rate is increasing. If interest rates begin to fall and you have your money in a money market, you give up the opportunity to lock up those high interest rates for a long period of time. If you had the ability to pick the direction of interest rates, the answer would be simple. Put your money in a money market when interest rates are going up and purchase long-term CDs or bonds as interest rates are coming down. Unfortunately, no one has a consistent record of picking the direction of interest rates. The solution is simple. Money markets are an excellent place to put the portion of your investments that require high liquidity or that are waiting to be committed to long-term investments.

Many retirees converted much of their investments to money markets in the early 1980s when interest rates were as high as 15 percent. As interest rates dropped, these same investors are currently receiving much less interest. This has caused a drastic decline in the amount of income they are receiving. In some cases, it has caused significant hardship. The moral is, once you have decided on the portion of your investment portfolio that should be in long-term fixed income investments, put it there. Don't try to be the wizard of Wall Street and play the interest rate game.

Money market funds now come in a variety of flavors. Some invest primarily in commercial paper and short-term certificates of deposit and normally pay the highest yield. For those investors who want absolute safety, there are funds that invest only in U.S. government treasury securities. They offer a slightly lower yield but the highest safety rating possible. For tax-conscious investors there are money market funds that offer tax-free interest. The investments made by these fund managers are in short-term securities issued by municipal and state governments. The interest rate paid by these funds is normally quite a bit lower than the other two; however, for the taxpayer in a higher bracket, it may be an attractive alternative.

TREASURY BILLS (T-BILLS)

If you want an investment with short maturity and the absolute in safety, your answer may be Treasury bills. T-bills are direct obligations of the U.S. government and are issued in four maturities; 91 days, 6 months, 9 months, and 1 year. The minimum investment in a Treasury bill is $10,000. They can be purchased through most banks, large brokerage firms, or even directly through the local branches of the Federal Reserve. Purchasing directly through the Federal Reserve is less convenient, but you save the $20 service fee.

New short-term Treasury bills are usually auctioned each week by the Federal Reserve. Nine-month and one-year bills are offered less often. The interest rate will vary each week depending on the changes of other interest rates in the economy. Once you have purchased a Treasury bill, your interest rate will be fixed until maturity. If you purchase a Treasury bill and need to liquidate it before its maturity, there is an active secondary market, and it can be sold.

T-bills have an unusual way of paying interest. Normally you would expect to deposit your $10,000 and at the maturity receive your $10,000 back plus interest. Treasury bills are different. They are sold at a discount. When you purchase a new Treasury bill, you do make the $10,000 deposit, but you are immediately refunded your interest. Your actual purchase price is $10,000 less prepaid interest. When the Treasury bill matures, you receive your full $10,000 face amount back. T-bills were formerly a popular investment among individual investors. Now with banks and savings and loans being free to offer competitive interest rates with their short-term CDs, it is more convenient to invest your money in them.

SAVINGS ACCOUNTS

For most of you, the first encounter with high finance was when your parents took you to a local bank or a savings and loan to open a savings account. Because you are so familiar with savings accounts and you have known about them for so long, almost every investor has one. The bankers love them, and well they should. The interest that you receive from a passbook savings account is normally very low compared to other alternative investments. Savings accounts do have some advantages. They can be opened with very minimum balances. Deposits or withdrawals can be made as many times as you would like during the month. The safety of savings accounts is very good. Usually deposits up to $100,000 are guaranteed by the FDIC (Federal Deposit Insurance Corporation) for banks, and by FSLIC (Federal Savings & Loan Insurance Corporation) for savings and loans. They are agencies of the federal government, therefore, your safety is AAA. Be a little careful on this point; some savings and loans and banks are state-chartered and they are insured by private insurance companies or by state insurance.

Why would anyone have a savings account? Hundreds of billions of dollars are currently invested in savings accounts paying very low rates of interest. In most cases, the investors are just too lazy or uninformed to seek out the better alternative investments. Fear of the unknown may also be a factor. Passbook savings accounts are a great place to teach children about how to save money. They are no place to invest.

CERTIFICATES OF DEPOSIT (CDs)

Over the last five or six years, the government has removed many restrictions on the way financial institutions do business. Probably no other area of the financial service business has become as competitive as banks and savings and loans attempting to attract long-term deposits. Long-term bank deposits or CDs have attracted substantial investor interest, especially among retired people.

When you invest in a certificate of deposit, you loan your money to the bank or savings and loan for a specific period of time. The length of your deposit can be as short as one month to as long as 10 to 12 years. Most banks and savings and loans have established a standard schedule for CD maturities. If your deposit is large enough, you can actually negotiate the exact maturity date of your certificate to suit your situation. When you invest in a certificate of deposit, you agree to leave your money with the financial institution until the maturity. Your banker knows how long he will have use of that money because you have given up your right to instant access of your money without a penalty. He is thus able to pay you a higher rate of interest than he would on a passbook account. The longer the maturity, the higher the yield.

What happens if you need your money before the maturity date on the certificate? That is no problem, but there are sacrifices. You can always "break" your certificate and get your money back. For banks that are insured by the FDIC and in savings and loans that are insured by the FSLIC, there are minimum penalties specified by the government. You should be aware that the financial institution can actually take part of your principal if your money has not been on deposit long enough to earn the interest to cover the penalty. Also, check with your specific bank or savings and loan to see what their penalties are. Each bank and savings and loan may impose greater penalties than those specified by the government.

Except for the penalties imposed for early withdrawal, there are almost no other risks associated with certificates of deposit of $100,000 or less because of FDIC or FSLIC insurance. There are still a few banks and savings and loans that are not covered by federal insurance. It may save you some sleepless nights to check first and make sure that your deposits are covered.

SHOP AROUND

It can really pay to shop around to get the best rate on your CDs. Remember the "gas wars" of the late 1960s and early 1970s? Each gas station on all four corners would lower the price of their gasoline in order to attract new customers. Well, there haven't been gas wars for a long time, but occasionally you will see outbreaks of CD wars. Once in a while, a new bank will open in an area and offer especially high rates on their CD's in order to attract deposits. Other banks in the area, in order to keep their depositors, often have to match those rates. You will find that the rate competition is normally with the short-term CDs of less than one year. If you happen to have funds that should be invested in CDs at that particular time, it can be attractive. Whether there is a banking war in your community or not, it is definitely worth shopping for the best CD rates.

WHERE 10 PERCENT IS BETTER THAN 10.5 PERCENT

With the removal of government restrictions, the banks and savings and loans now have a great deal of flexibility in the investments they offer. Is a three-year CD at 10 percent at Federal Bank as good as a 10.5 percent CD at National Bank? Maybe. It depends on how often they compound your interest. If you make a $10,000 deposit at National Bank where they're paying you 10.5 percent but compound it once a year, you will receive a $1,050 credit to your account at the end of the first year. If you make the same deposit at the Federal Bank where they are paying only 10 percent, but compounding daily, they will credit your account for one day's interest each day. On the second day your money is invested, you receive interest on your $10,000 deposit plus the amount of interest that was credited the day before. On the third day, you receive interest on your original deposit plus the two days' previous interest, and so on. At the end of one year, you would earn $1,052 interest on your $10,000 deposit which is more than the interest earned at 10.5 percent without the advantage of daily compounding. This is called interest compounding. It can make a significant difference on the "effective annual yield" of your CD. Before you make a deposit, be sure to ask your banker what effective annual yield he pays. The chart below will help you sort out the results of various methods of compounding.

Effective Annual Yield		
	CD Rate	
8 Percent	*10 Percent*	*12 Percent*
Compounded:		
annually 8.000	10.000	12.000
quarterly 8.243	10.381	12.551
monthly 8.300	10.471	12.683
daily 8.328	10.516	12.748

SAVINGS BONDS (EE BONDS)

U.S. savings bonds have not traditionally provided a very good form of investment. In fact, up until recently, the interest rates they paid were not competitive. That has changed and the advantages are these: As with other U.S. government bonds, the principal and interest are absolutely free from risk. In addition, the interest received on U.S. savings bonds is not subject to taxation by state and local governments. Also, while their interest is taxable for federal tax purposes, you are not taxed on that interest until you redeem the bond. This allows you to accumulate a nice nest egg on a tax-deferred basis without the risk of principal. They provide good liquidity although you may have to give up some interest. The government will redeem your savings bond at any time after you have held it for six months. During the second six months, it will be redeemed at a lower interest rate, normally 5.5 percent. The longer the bond is held, the higher interest you receive.

The interest now paid on U.S. savings bonds is quite competitive. You are guaranteed a minimum of $7\frac{1}{2}$ percent or 85 percent of the average yield on the five-year Treasury notes. Naturally, with the same safety, you can get the higher yield by actually buying the five-year Treasury note.

As mentioned earlier, it is important to have some of your funds invested so that you can get to them quickly. No matter which of these investments you choose, they will serve your purpose. My choice is money market mutual funds or money market accounts. They pay a fair rate of interest which will always remain competitive with other similar investments. Their safety factor is very high and they are extremely convenient.

The next group of investments are those that provide a high, stable rate of return. For most retirees, this is where a majority of your money will be invested.

Fixed-Income Investments

Have you ever heard the phrase "I don't know where the next dollar is coming from"? For retirees, that can be pretty scary. That's why high-yielding, fixed income investments should make up a bulk of the investment portfolio for the retiree. These investments are designed to pay a high, consistent rate of return month after month. Some of the investments pay income that is fully taxable while others have significant tax advantages. The six fixed-income investments we will cover are corporate bonds, long-term U.S. treasury securities, tax-free municipal bonds, zero-coupon bonds, annuities, and preferred stocks.

CORPORATE BONDS

Corporate bonds are considered a conservative investment offering a high, fixed income with low risk. When a large corporation needs money for the purposes of expansion or new business development, it has several sources. It could sell stock or it could borrow the money. If the corporation decided that borrowing money was the best alternative, it could go to a bank if it only needed the money for up to a year or so. But if the corporation needed the money for a longer period of time, it would borrow from investors.

A corporate bond is simply a loan agreement between you

(the lender) and the corporation (the borrower). If you're going to lend money, you will want to know when you will get it back, what interest you will receive, and how safe the loan is. Those things are covered in the loan agreement. The corporation will tell you the exact date that they will repay the full amount of the loan. This is known as the maturity date. If the corporation feels that they will need the money for only a short period of time, they may issue bonds that have a maturity date of just five years. If, on the other hand, the need for money is for a long-term project, the maturity date may be as long as 30 years.

Secured and Unsecured Bonds

The safety of your investment depends on several factors. Is the loan you have made to the corporation secured or unsecured? Mortgage bonds are secured loans. They are secured by a specific corporate asset. If the company were to default on the loan, the bondholders can take the asset and sell it to recover their money.

If the bond is unsecured, it's called a debenture. There is no specific asset of the corporation that secures this loan. Instead, you depend upon the earning power and other assets of the corporation to repay the loan. Naturally, debentures carry a little more risk and offer a little more return.

Your bond (the loan agreement) will also state the principal amount of the loan. Bonds are usually issued in $1,000 minimum denominations. For each $1,000 principal, the corporation guarantees to repay you the $1,000 on the maturity date.

The bond certificate will also tell you the amount of interest you will receive. The interest is quoted as a percentage of the principal or "par value." If the rate stated on the bond (the nominal yield) is 12½ percent, you will receive $125 per year for each $1,000 par value bond you hold.

You will receive your interest check from the corporation on specific dates stated in the agreement. Interest payments are normally made every six months. As an example, suppose you invested $10,000 in a corporate bond with a 10 percent nominal yield and a maturity date of January 15, 1995. You would expect to receive interest payments every six months, normally on January 15th and July 15th of each year. These interest payments would be $500 each ($1,000 for the year). On January 15th, 1995, you would receive your entire $10,000 back as repayment of the loan by the corporation.

Sound good? You make a loan to a big corporation, and they send you a check every six months for a high rate of interest. It is a good investment for a conservative investor looking for high income.

Does this mean you have to call General Motors when you have some money to invest and negotiate a loan with them? No, not at all. When a corporation like General Motors decides it needs to raise money through a bond issue, they usually need very large amounts. General Motors may issue $100 million worth of bonds at a time. Naturally, there are not a lot of individuals who have $100 million to lend to General Motors. General Motors will work with an investment banker to structure a loan arrangement that will meet their needs but, at the same time, offer a yield high enough to attract the attention of individual investors. When the interest rate and maturity date have been agreed upon, the investment banking firm will use the services of the many stock brokerage firms to help find investors for these bonds. Each investor who purchases the bonds in the $1,000 increments (there may be thousands of investors in each bond) has exactly the same loan agreement with General Motors.

How about Liquidity?

Suppose you need to get your money back before the maturity date. That can be easily accomplished. Most large bond issues of major corporations have an active secondary market. Your bond can be sold to another investor quickly and easily through most stock brokerage firms.

Who will buy the bond from you? Another investor who is looking for a safe investment that has high, fixed income. How much will you get paid for your bond? Good question. You may get more or less than your original $1,000 investment back. It depends on the level of interest rates at the time.

Suppose that when you purchased a newly issued bond 10 percent was considered a fair interest rate. Your bond had 10 percent nominal yield which means for every $1,000 you invested, you get $100 per year. Now, let's suppose that because of economic changes, interest rates have gone up. Prevailing rates on corporate bonds are now 15 percent. This means that the same corporation issuing bonds with the same maturity date and the same safety factor would have to pay investors 15 percent instead of 10 percent. Therefore, an investor purchasing a newly issued corporate bond would receive a 15 percent interest rate. That is $150 per year for each $1,000 invested. Any investor offered a choice between receiving $100 per year on your older corporate bond or $150 a year by investing in a new corporate bond would obviously choose the new bond.

The investor might be willing to buy your bond if you lowered the price. You would have to lower it enough so that the new investor felt he or she was getting as good a deal as investing in the 15 percent bond. What price is that? I will show you how to figure it.

Current Yield

Current yield is the percentage cash return you receive each year. It is calculated by dividing the interest received each year by the value of the bond. As an example, a bond that paid $100 per year in interest and that could be purchased for $667 would get the same current yield as a bond paying $150 per year which cost $1,000 ($100/667 = 15 percent; $150/1000 = 15 percent).

An investor may be willing to pay you $667 per bond which would offer him the same current yield that he could get by purchasing the new bond.

You would then have to decide whether you wanted to go ahead and liquidate the bond at a loss or sell some other asset to raise the money you needed.

Not all the news is bad. Suppose, on the other hand, that after you purchased your 10 percent corporate bond, interest rates came down to where corporations only had to pay 7½ percent interest or $75 per year on each $1,000 bond. You now have a valuable asset. You have a loan agreement with a major corporation that will pay you $100 per year for every $1,000 invested. If you wanted to sell your bond today, you would get more than $1,000. Using the same logic as the above example, an investor may be willing to pay you $1,333 for your $1,000 bond ($100/$1333 = 7½ percent).

Both of the above examples are simplistic. Other factors need to be considered in determining what the future price of a bond might be. These factors include the credit rating of the bond and the number of years remaining to maturity. The important thing to know is that bonds are liquid. You can sell them if you need to get your money. The price that you sell them for will depend on what current interest rates are at the time. You may be liquidating your bonds for a profit or a loss.

How about Safety?

How safe are corporate bonds? That really depends on the financial stability of the corporation issuing those bonds. A bond issued by a company like General Motors or a large utility like Southern California Edison is going to be a lot safer than a bond issued by a small unknown company. To assist investors in evaluating the risk of bond investments Standard & Poor's and Moody's, two independent rating services, evaluate the credit rating of each corporation. Each bond is given a rating that may change from time to time. The four highest ratings of each service are as follows:

> Standard & Poor's: AAA, AA, A, BBB
> Moody's: Aaa, Aa, A, Baa

There are lower ratings issued but they should not be considered for investment. The lower ratings would be for corporations with less solid financial situations. If you consider corporate bonds as an investment, do not invest in any that have a rating less than A. Don't be lured by the slightly higher rates of return that you may be able to obtain on less than investment-quality bonds. It's just not worth the additional risk. The interest received on corporate bonds is subject to state and federal income tax as ordinary income.

If you are considering the purchase of corporate bonds,

the most practical method is in a mutual fund or a unit trust. They provide you the opportunity for diversification by owning a number of different bonds in the portfolio. They offer the convenience of receiving a check every month, every quarter, or every six months as you desire, as well as the benefit of professional management.

LONG-TERM U.S. TREASURY SECURITIES

Corporations are not the only ones who have to borrow money from time to time. One of the largest issuers of bonds is the U.S. government. U.S. government bonds are very similar to corporate bonds. They are normally issued in $1,000 amounts with maturity dates typically ranging between 5 and 20 years. The interest you receive is paid every six months at the fixed rate stated on the bond certificate. The interest rate on a U.S. government bond is going to be less than a corporate bond because they are considered safer. All U.S. government securities are rated AAA. The security behind the U.S. bonds is the full faith, credit, and taxing power (which we know can be substantial) of the United States government. A U.S. government guarantee is considered the safest investment that you can make.

If you need to sell your bonds before the maturity date, you can. Like corporate bonds, there is a very active secondary market for government bonds. Once again, you do not know exactly what price you will receive as that will depend upon current interest rates at the time you want to make the sale. You may receive more or less than you paid for the bonds. The interest you receive on your U.S. government bonds is subject to federal income taxes as ordinary income but not subject to state income tax.

Ginnie Maes

That sounds like a funny name for an investment. If your name was Government National Mortgage Association Modified Pass Through Certificate, you would shorten it too. Ginnie Maes (GNMAs) are a little bit different than other government securities, but they have become very popular with individual investors. They are popular because you can usually earn about .5 percent more on Ginnie Maes than on other medium-term U.S. government securities even though they carry the same AAA guarantee. They are particularly attractive to pension plan investors and retirees because of their high safety and high yield.

The Government National Mortgage Association (GNMA) was established as an agency of the federal government under the Housing and Urban Development Act of 1968. GNMA purchases large quantities of FHA and VA single or multifamily mortgages and pools them together. When you invest in a GNMA, you are purchasing a proportionate share of that pool of mortgages. In effect, you are making an investment much like a bank when they lend money to someone buying a home. Each month, GNMA collects the mortgage payments and then pays it out proportionately to the owners of the GNMA pool (less a small fee). Just like a bank, when you receive these mortgage payments, most of the money you receive is interest, but a small portion is principal. When you receive the monthly check from GNMA, the amount that is principal and the amount that is interest is identified on the check.

The maturities on most FHA and VA mortgages are 30 years. However, the practical life, or maturity, of a GNMA pass-through certificate is 12 or 13 years. This shorter maturity takes place because of the mobility of the American population. When houses are sold with FHA and VA mortgages, normally those loans are paid off. When the loans are repaid, you, as a mortgage certificate holder, receive a proportionate share of the principal back. By the end of 12 or 13 years, most of the houses are sold or the loans have been repaid.

As an agency of the U.S. government, the GNMA guarantee is backed by the U.S. Treasury. GNMA has the full authority to borrow as much as it needs from the U.S. Treasury to meet any of the obligations. GNMA, therefore, guarantees the repayment of all principal and interest. If any mortgage borrowers fail to make their mortgage payments, GNMA can call upon the U.S. Treasury to make that payment to the investor.

When new GNMA mortgage-backed certificates are issued, they are in minimum denominations of $25,000. You can, however, purchase older GNMA units for less than $25,000 because some of the mortgage principal has already been repaid. There is an active secondary market for GNMA units so they can be sold easily. Like other bonds, you may receive more or less than what you paid. They can normally be sold through any brokerage firm with the proceeds paid to you within five business days.

One possible drawback to GNMAs is that some principal is repaid each month. If you are not careful, you find yourself spending these small principal checks as they come in and are left with nothing at maturity. It is important that you reinvest the principal in a money market fund or other investment so as not to inadvertently spend that principal.

The most convenient and practical method of purchasing GNMAs is through the unit trust or mutual fund. By doing this, they will automatically reinvest the principal for you, so you are not tempted to spend it.

GNMAs are particularly attractive to people in retirement because they do pay their interest each month as opposed to every six months like other government bonds. Monthly payments are made to certificate holders on the 15th of the month.

TAX-FREE BONDS

Due to tax bracket creep and other reasons, more and more Americans are looking for ways to invest money so their return is not taxed. People with income that may be considered modest can end up paying more than 25 cents of every dollar to the U.S. government. State and local taxes take an additional portion of those earnings. There is no wonder that the avoidance of income taxes has become one of the major investment objectives of American investors.

Municipal Bonds

A municipal bond is similar in many ways to both corporate and government bonds. When you invest in municipal bonds, you are making the loan to an American state, municipality, or other local government agency. Municipal bonds make interest payments every six months, and repay your principal at a specific date in the future (maturity date).

Why would a local government issue bonds? It's done all the time for various reasons. Take the situation of a county wanting to build a new school. The school district knows it can pay for the new school buildings from the property taxes collected in the future from the residents of its district. In order for the school to be built now, municipal bonds are issued and sold to investors. The proceeds from the bond sale are used to build the school buildings. The county school district will then use the taxes collected on real estate properties to repay the interest and the principal on the bonds. Municipal bond issues are used to finance new roads, airports, and other projects needed by state, city, and county governments.

The maturities on municipal bonds can range from as short as a few months to as long as 30 or 40 years. Naturally, the longer the maturity, the higher interest rate you will receive.

One special feature that sets municipal bonds apart from both corporate and government bonds is that all the interest received by the investors is federal income tax-free. It is also not subject to state income taxes if the bonds are issued by a municipality within the state in which you live. The tax exemption of interest income on municipals is based on the principle of "reciprocal immunity." This simply means that the U.S. government may not tax the states nor may the states tax the federal government.

The tax-free nature of municipal bond interest is one main reason for the popularity of municipal bonds. A short example can illustrate how important this advantage is. If you invest in a certificate of deposit at the bank and receive 10 percent interest which is fully taxable, your after-tax return would be only 7.5 percent if you were in the 25 percent bracket. How does that work? Assume you invest $10,000 in the CD at 10 percent; your interest payment each year would be $1,000. If you had to pay $250 (25 percent) of your interest to the federal government in taxes, you would be left with just $750. $750 is 7½ percent of your $10,000 investment.

TABLE 8-1
Taxable Equivalents
Rate of Return

Tax Bracket	7.00%	8.00%	9.00%	10.00%	11.00%	12.00%
20.00%	8.75%	10.00%	11.25%	12.50%	13.75%	15.00%
25.00	9.33	10.67	12.00	13.33	14.67	16.00
30.00	10.00	11.43	12.86	14.29	15.71	17.14
35.00	10.77	12.31	13.85	15.38	16.92	18.46
40.00	11.67	13.33	15.00	16.67	18.33	20.00
45.00	12.73	14.55	16.36	18.18	20.00	21.82
50.00	14.00	16.00	18.00	20.00	22.00	24.00

Naturally, this doesn't include the possibility of having to pay state income taxes on the interest also.

If that same $10,000 were invested in a municipal bond yielding 10 percent, you would keep the entire $1,000 interest payment each year. None of that would be subject to federal or state income taxes. Look at it from another angle. Suppose you are in the 25 percent tax bracket and have the opportunity to invest in a 10 percent municipal bond or a 12 percent government bond. Which one would be better? The easiest way to make this comparison is to calculate the taxable equivalent for the municipal bond yield. It may sound complicated, but it's really very easy. Take the rate of return available on the tax-free municipal bond and divide it by the reciprocal of your tax bracket. The reciprocal is calculated by subtracting your tax bracket from one. In our illustration that is 1 − .25 = .75. Now, divide 10 percent by .75 and you get 13.33 percent. This means that to achieve the same after-tax return as a 10 percent tax-free municipal bond, you would need to get 13.33 percent in a taxable bond or CD. You can now understand why municipal bonds are such a popular investment for people in higher tax brackets. Table 8-1 will show you the taxable equivalent returns necessary based on various tax brackets.

In addition to the tax advantages, municipal bonds with high ratings are considered extremely safe second only to

U.S. government securities. Naturally, the safety of each individual municipal bond is based on the particular project that is being financed and the financial strength of the municipality.

Two Kinds of Municipal Bonds

Municipal bonds fall into two categories. General obligation bonds are backed by the full taxing power of the municipality. Revenue bonds are issued for a specific purpose, normally to build a specific facility such as an airport. The revenues generated from that facility, such as landing fees, are pledged to the repayment of the principal and interest on the municipal bond.

To assist investors in determining the quality and safety of municipal bonds, they are rated by the two independent rating services, Moody's and Standard & Poor's. Ratings of the two services will rank from the best quality, AAA, down to the lowest quality rank, C. I would recommend not purchasing municipal bonds with a quality rating lower than A.

Like other bonds, municipal bonds have an active secondary market. Should you decide that you need to liquidate your municipal bond investment, it can normally be accomplished very quickly and easily through any of the major stock brokerage houses. The proceeds from your sale are available within five business days. Like other bonds, you may receive more or less than you paid.

Investors in municipal bonds should be cautioned against investing in very small bond issues unless they intend to hold the bonds to maturity. The smaller bond issues may be good quality but the secondary market normally is not very active, which means they could be hard to sell.

To further enhance the safety of municipal bonds, some have the payment of principal and interest insured. With an insured bond, both the principal and interest is guaranteed by a consortium of the large insurance companies. Insured bonds carry a AAA rating.

Unless you have enough money to purchase a diversified portfolio of municipal bonds, your best bet is to purchase a unit trust or mutual fund. By doing this, you have not only professional management, but also are invested in a diversified portfolio of bonds. In most cases, you can purchase a unit trust where the whole portfolio is insured and thus ranked AAA in safety. In addition, many unit trusts will be comprised of municipal bonds of just one state. This allows residents of that state to not only avoid federal income taxes but state income taxes also.

ZERO-COUPON BONDS (ZEROS)

While not very attractive for retired investors, zero-coupon bonds have become popular. Like other corporate, municipal, or government bonds, they are normally issued for long maturities, usually 10 to 30 years. Unlike other bonds, they do not pay interest until maturity.

Why would anybody invest in something where they did not receive any interest for as much as 30 years? "Zeros" offer an interesting opportunity to take advantage of compound interest. You purchase a zero at a significant discount from its redemption value. As it matures, you are actually earning the interest, but you are not receiving it. As an example, if you purchased a zero-coupon bond that matured in 30 years and yielded 10 percent interest, you would pay just over $53. That's right. A bond that will pay you $1,000 in 30 years only costs you $53.54 today. That's the power of compound interest. Not only do you have the opportunity of locking in a high yield, you are also locking in the rate your interest is compounding.

The zero-coupon bond is not normally a good choice for the retired investor as they carry a double negative. You do not receive any interest during the life of the investment with which to meet living expenses. The IRS, however, requires that you pay taxes on the interest that accrues to you each year. What does all that mean? You will earn interest and will have to pay taxes on it, but you will not actually receive any cash income. This is negative cash flow and not normally what the retired investor is looking for.

There is one aspect of the zero-coupon bond that can be attractive for the retiree. In many cases, investors will want to put aside some money to provide for the college education expenses of their grandchildren. A zero-coupon bond can be purchased at a significant discount and gifted to the grand- child. You can select a maturity date that will correspond to the year that your grandchild starts college. In this way, a significant amount of money will be available when college tuition comes due. Because you have gifted the bond to your grandchild, taxes due on the accruing interest are paid at the grandchild's tax bracket, which will normally be lower than yours.

You can buy zero-coupon bonds in three varieties; those backed by corporate securities, those backed by government securities, and those backed by tax-free municipal securities. There is no federal income tax liability on those backed by municipal securities, but the interest rate will be lower.

SINGLE PREMIUM ANNUITIES

In the early 1970s, the single premium deferred annuity be- came the rage of Wall Street. It provided a very safe invest- ment at competitive interest rates and offered the advantage of tax deferral. An annuity is an investment made with an insurance company. They can be purchased, however, through stock brokerage firms as well as insurance represen- tatives. The single premium deferred annuity is a life insur- ance policy but can be thought of as a loan made to the insurance company. The interest rate you receive from the insurance company is normally competitive with other in- terest rates available.

The main advantage is the tax-deferral benefit. As long as you do not withdraw the interest earned, you do not have to pay any current federal or state income taxes on that interest. This allows your money to compound at attractive interest rates on a pre-tax basis. Because of this tax deferral feature, they are very popular with investors who are still in higher tax brackets. These investors can usually afford to allow the interest to remain on deposit and compound because they don't need it for living expenses. Annuities come in every shape, size, and variety. They are generally very safe. Usually with some small penalty provision, you can get your money back when you want it. Information can be obtained from any of the major stock brokerage firms, major life insurance companies, or your financial planner.

Single Premium Whole Life Insurance

Most insurance policies require that you pay premiums year after year. Like its name, single premium whole life is a life insurance policy where you make only one premium payment at the beginning. Normally, insurance policies of this type are for a minimum of $10,000 or more. Like other insurance policies, it does pay a death benefit. Usually, this benefit is somewhat greater than the cash value of the policy. There are several features with this life insurance policy that make it particularly attractive as an investment for the retired investor.

Safety. With most policies of this type, you are always guaranteed to get 100 percent of your principal back. This guarantee is made by the life insurance company, so you should be sure to select policies from high-quality companies. This guarantee of principal repayment makes this investment safer than bonds because the prices of bonds can fluctuate with interest rates.

Yield. Normally, the insurance company will establish the interest rate they will pay on the policy once a year. This interest rate can fluctuate and usually is somewhat above the current money market rates. If you are in a period of rising interest rates, life insurance companies will normally increase the rate paid on these policies in order to keep their customers.

Tax Advantages. Like other insurance policies, as long as you leave the interest earned in the policy, there is no current tax on that interest. If you surrender the policy, however, you immediately have a tax liability on the entire amount of interest accumulated.

Borrowing Ability. Like other whole life policies, you have the ability to borrow against the value of the policy. If you borrow from the policy, the amount that you borrow is not considered a surrender and, therefore, is not taxed. By borrowing out the interest earned each year, you have the same effect as a tax-free income. If you should die with the policy in force, your beneficiary would receive the total accumulated value of your policy less the amount that you borrowed. The law provides that this would be received by the beneficiary at a stepped up cost basis, which simply means that all the accumulated interest would escape income taxes.

PREFERRED STOCKS

The preferred stock takes some of the disadvantages of corporate bonds, adds them to some of the disadvantages of common stocks, and combines them to make one relatively unattractive investment for the individual investor. As an individual investor in a preferred stock, you are entitled to a fixed dividend yearly. In that sense, the preferred stock is very much like other fixed-income investments. Even though owners of preferred stocks are considered owners of the company, they usually do not have all of the privileges of common stockholders. In most cases, they cannot vote at the annual meetings. If the company does well, the board of directors may vote an increased dividend to the common stockholders, but the preferred stockholders are stuck with their same fixed dividend amount. On the other hand, if the company does very poorly, the board of directors may vote not to pay the preferred stock dividend.

There is little appreciation potential with the preferred stock. The dividends are fixed much like the interest payment on a bond so the price will tend to change based on changes in interest rates.

As the name indicates, the preferred stockholders do get preferential treatment in some circumstances. Dividends to preferred stockholders must be paid before any dividends can be paid to common stockholders. In the event of a liquidation of the company, the preferred stockholders get their money back before the common stockholders. Interest payments to bondholders, however, must be paid before preferred dividends. In addition, the claim of bondholders exceeds that of the preferred stockholders in case of a corporate liquidation.

FIGURE 8-1
Mutual Funds and Unit Trusts

Income—Mutual Funds

Fidelity Puritan 800-225-6666	No load
National Securities Total Return 800-522-4022	Load
Valueline Income 800-223-0818	No load
Decatur Income 800-523-4640	Load

Government Bond—Mutual Funds

Vanguard Fixed Income 800-662-7447	No load
Kemper U.S. Government Securities 800-621-1048	No load
Franklin U.S. Government Securities 800-632-2350	Load

Municipal Bond—Mutual Funds

Colonial Tax Exempt High Yield 800-225-2365	Load
Vanguard Muni Bond High Yield 800-662-7447	No load
Merrill Lynch High Yield 800-282-2000	Load
Dreyfus Tax Exempt Bond 800-645-6561	No load

Municipal Bonds—Unit Trusts

First Trust (Clayton Brown)
800-282-9558

Nuveen
Florida   800-223-3996
National   800-225-2688

Van Kampen Merritt
National   800-826-5267

As you can see, there really isn't much reason to invest in preferred stocks, with a couple of possible exceptions. If you happen to own a corporation, 85 percent of the dividends you receive from preferred and common stocks are not taxable to your corporation. Preferred stocks do offer a relatively safe, high after-tax yield investment to corporate investors, both large and small.

The other possible exception is with the convertible preferred stock. Like other preferreds, the convertible preferred will pay an attractive, fixed dividend. However, owners of the convertible have the privilege of converting their shares of their preferred stock into shares of the common stock if it becomes attractive. This normally allows you the higher safety factor of owning a preferred stock because of its prior claims on dividends and assets, as well as the appreciation potential of the common stock if the company does well.

Since most retirees depend on their investments to pay a consistent rate of return, they should have at least 50 percent of their investment portfolio in fixed-income securities. A short list of mutual funds and unit trusts that specialize in each of these areas is listed in Figure 8–1. The list is not intended to be exhaustive but it does cover many of the large companies, including their phone numbers where you can get additional information.

CHAPTER NINE

Growth Investments

In the early chapters of this book, we discussed inflation. It can be the one real enemy of the retired investor. The way of overcoming that investment enemy is to have a portion of your investments placed in areas that actually benefit from inflation. These investments are made up of assets you own, as opposed to fixed-income investments in which you have made a loan. The two most common, and probably the most suitable growth-oriented investments, are common stocks and real estate.

COMMON STOCKS

Opinion has rarely been more divided. Some investors feel that common stocks offer the best investment opportunity of the free enterprise system. Others feel that participation in the ownership of common stocks is tantamount to a trip to Las Vegas, except that Las Vegas is more fun. Which of these two opinions you have probably depends on whether you have made or lost money in the stock market. Certainly fortunes have been made and fortunes have been lost in the stock market and they will continue to be in the future. We are not here to discuss how to make a fortune and certainly not how to lose one, but rather how to obtain an above-average rate of return on your investments. For a portion of your investment portfolio, common stocks can offer an excellent investment for long-term growth.

If you have not invested in common stocks before, don't be intimidated. Investment in common stocks can offer you a very attractive return and there are methods of participating in the stock market that don't require your expertise.

Two Reasons to Own Common Stocks

1. To obtain current income through high dividends that will increase in the future.
2. To obtain growth of your principal so that its value will be maintained despite inflation.

What Is a Common Stock?

Common stocks represent a share of the ownership in a corporation. As a shareholder, you are entitled to a voice in the affairs of your company. You can make your voice heard by voting on the affairs of the company at the annual meetings that, as the name implies, are held once a year.

Dividends

In addition to your voting rights, you are also entitled to a proportionate share of the dividend payment authorized by the board of directors. Most corporations pay dividends once every quarter, although there is no requirement that they do so. The amount of the dividend depends on the profitability of the company and the philosophy of the board of directors. Some companies pay out a majority of their corporate profits to the stockholder. Others pay out nothing and retain the money to invest in further expansion of the company.

The common stock of some companies offers excellent inflation hedges for the investor. As inflation causes prices to increase, the company will usually receive higher prices for the products it sells. This will cause profits to increase and provide more money than can be paid out as dividends. Dividend increases do not always depend on inflation. If you invest in a successful company, it will grow. This growth will produce additional profits for dividends. This is one reason that we regard common stocks as growth investments. Rather than income that is fixed, the dividends from common stocks can increase.

Before you get too excited here, the opposite can also be true. If the company is not successful and does not earn a profit, not only do you have the potential of not getting any dividends but you also run the risk of losing your principal if your stock declines in value. Normally companies that pay high dividend yields are more mature companies whose prospects for rapid growth are not as great. Dividend yields on common stocks of mature companies currently range up as high as 10 percent for good-quality industrial and utility companies.

Appreciation

The other benefit offered by common stocks is the possibility of growth in your investment asset itself. Suppose you invest in a share of stock at $10 per share because you feel the company will be successful. If the company does become more successful and doubles its profits, you can expect the price of your share to double in value to $20. (Actually, it is a bit more complicated, but the theory is the same.)

Probably the most confusing thing about common stocks is the stock market itself. It is an emotional animal. The price fluctuations of a common stock, both up and down, are determined by what investors think the future of the company holds. If they think the future is good, they buy more of the stock and cause the price to go up. If they think the future looks bad, they will sell their shares causing the price to go down. What makes it interesting is not everyone agrees on the future.

Two Reasons Stock Prices Change

While there is logic behind how the prices of common stocks change, that's not the whole story. Because people are emotional, the stock market and the prices of individual common stocks are often influenced by two emotions: fear and greed.

When prospects for a company start to look bright, investors often become overly optimistic (greedy). As they buy more shares, this causes the price of the stock to go much higher than is realistic. On the other hand, sometimes bad news or a poor business decision will cause investors to become overly negative on the future prospects for their company and cause some to sell. As the price declines, others become afraid of losing more money and they sell. As more and more people sell, the stock drops farther and farther.

In 1978 and 1979, we had two good examples of both these emotions. Many new casinos were anticipated to open in Atlantic City, New Jersey. Before the casinos of Resorts International and Caesars World and others were built, stock prices of these companies were soaring. Naturally, no profits had been earned yet, but investors anticipated large profits. After all, wouldn't everybody from New York, New Jersey, and the whole Eastern seaboard flock to Atlantic City to gamble? All of the casinos would earn great profits and all the stockholders would benefit. The prices of these stocks became very volatile and skyrocketed. It would have been very easy for an investor to be caught up in the emotion of the moment and buy those stocks. Now the casinos are open and, in most cases, they are operating at a profit. The stock prices, however, are now down 50 percent to 75 percent of the highs that they reached during that emotional period.

In 1979, a McDonnell Douglas DC10 crashed outside of Chicago with all passengers killed. The common stock in McDonnell Douglas, which had been selling at around $30 a share, dropped in a few days to around $18. Fear had set in. After all, maybe nobody would ride DC10s again. Therefore, no airline would buy any more of the planes from McDonnell Douglas, thus decreasing their profits. What about the potential for lawsuits from the families of all the passengers? The outlook seemed grim. As many investors rushed to sell their stock, the price dropped. There were a few astute investors who stepped in to buy those shares. Those investors saw past the emotion of the moment and knew that if McDonnell Douglas never made or sold another DC10, the assets of the company were worth far more than $18 a share.

Within a few days, the panic was over and the stock began to climb back up. By 1985, it traded for over $80 a share.

The Value of Common Stocks

What's the bottom-line recommendation on common stocks? Common stocks offer a good investment opportunity for a portion of your growth-oriented assets. Investing in common stocks, however, is not for the novice. Even if you are astute at analyzing the future prospects for an individual company, you never know how the stock market is going to react. Delegate the decision making of which common stocks to buy and sell to the professionals.

If you have substantial assets, you can employ a personal money manager or investment adviser to watch after your portfolio. If, however, you are like most and your assets are limited, you should consider a mutual fund. Many mutual funds offer very good long-term investment results, but you have to pick and choose. Look for a mutual fund that has a long-term track record of success. There are a number of mutual funds that have a track record averaging over 20 percent a year over a 10-year period for their investors. Be sure that you look at the long-term track record of 10 years. There are many mutual funds available and not all of them have had good performance. Don't get caught up in the success of a specialized mutual fund because of a one- or two-year track record. Concentrate on looking for long-term results.

Mutual funds offer you the opportunity to participate in a diversified portfolio with a relatively small amount of money. You have the advantages of professional management, experienced people who understand the stock market. A mutual fund is a passive investment. You don't have to worry about the day-to-day fluctuations. Use your retirement years as an opportunity to take strokes off your golf game. Do not add to the number of sleepless nights you may have had during your working years.

Select a mutual fund whose stated objective fits your need. There are many that are conservative which invest in high-dividend, blue-chip stocks. These can offer both good current income as well as appreciation.

REAL ESTATE

"Real estate is a good investment. They ain't making any more of the stuff." Will Rogers was certainly correct in that they're not making any more real estate. But, that fact alone doesn't make it a good investment. The above-average rate of return available in real estate is not just a matter of luck. Proper real estate investment requires considerable experience and thorough analysis. The fact that they are no longer making additional swampland in Florida or desert in Nevada, doesn't necessarily make it a good investment.

Properly selected real estate, over the years, has probably produced a better long-term rate of return than any other investment. Because of this track record real estate may provide the retired investor with a good alternative for a growth-oriented investment.

Investment real estate (that is, real estate other than your own home) can be broken down into several major categories: raw land, residential rental properties, and commercial properties.

Raw Land

If you invest in raw land, you are purchasing property that has no buildings or development on it. You are hoping to buy the land cheaply and, at some time in the future, sell it for a substantial profit. This can normally be done when the land can then be used for building houses, shopping centers, offices, or other development. Investment in raw land is very speculative; you may have to wait a very long time before the land can be sold at a profit. During that time you are not receiving any cash return. If you are wrong about its desirability for future buildings, you lose the use of your money for the period of time you own the land. It's also possible that you will have to sell the land for less than you paid for it. Even if you pay for the land with all cash, you will have yearly expenses for property tax. Investing in raw land is normally not suitable for the retired investor.

Residential Rental Properties

Residential rental properties are normally single-family houses or duplexes. If you are good at selecting properties and astute enough to buy them for the right price, residential rental properties can provide a very attractive investment return. The basic idea is to purchase a single-family house and rent it on a month-to-month basis for use by somebody else. The rental income normally covers your mortgage payments if your down payment has been large enough. As inflation causes other prices to rise, you can raise the rents. This will provide you with a higher cash return as well as making the property more valuable to a future buyer. At some time in the future, you can sell the property, hopefully, for a profit. As usual, there's no free lunch. Many people have tried their hand at managing residential rental properties. Very few of them try it a second time. It takes a lot of work to keep the properties rented and maintained. Some people find it very difficult to tell an unemployed father with a wife and two children that he has to move out because he can't pay his rent.

Commercial Properties

Commercial properties are normally large office buildings, shopping centers, and warehouses. Most investors, unless they have a lot of money, are not able to participate in these types of real estate investments on their own. These properties are normally purchased by large insurance companies, banks, pension plans, very large investors, or partnerships. For most individual investors, the best, and possibly the only way to participate in a large commercial property investment is through a limited partnership.

Why Is Real Estate a Good Investment?

Why has real estate provided such a good long-term rate of return? Why is it so popular with individual investors? A look at some hypothetical numbers will make the answer evident. Assume you purchase a large office building for $1,000,000 in cash. If you rent all the space available in the building (100 percent occupancy), you may collect $150,000 a year (gross rents). As owner of the building, you have certain expenses such as keeping the lawns mowed, maintaining the building, paying insurance, paying taxes, and the like. The expenses on your building may be $50,000 a year. That leaves a profit (net operating income) of $100,000 per year.

Gross rents	$150,000
Operating expenses	− 50,000
Net operating income	$100,000

That gives you a 10 percent cash return on your $1,000,000 investment ($100,000 divided by $1,000,000 = 10 percent).

A 10 percent per year return is not bad but there's a lot more. If inflation is running at 7 percent a year, you can expect to raise the rents at that same rate. It also means that your expenses of operating the building are also increasing at 7 percent per year. As you can see from Table 9–1, in the second year, you collect rents of $160,500. Your expenses are $53,500, which means your net operating income in the second year is $107,000. So, in the second year, you have earned a 10.7 percent cash return on your original $1,000,000 investment. You have no interest expense because you paid all cash for the building.

Following the table, you see in the fifth year, you will be collecting rents of $196,619. Expenses in that year will be $65,540, leaving you a net operating income of $131,080. That is approximately 13 percent cash return on your $1,000,000 investment.

Inflation is the friend of the real estate owner. It provides the opportunity to increase rents. The higher the inflation rate, the faster the rents can be increased. Even though expenses are also rising, you receive an increasing return. Real estate can provide the retired investor with an increasing income in order to meet increasing living expenses.

The advantages don't stop here. Inflation causes the value of the property itself to increase. Assuming the same 7 per-

TABLE 9-1

	Year 1	Year 2	Year 3	Year 4	Year 5
Rent income	$150,000	$160,500	$171,735	$183,756	$196,619
Expenses	50,000	53,500	57,245	61,252	65,540
Net operating income	$100,000	$107,000	$114,490	$122,504	$131,080
Interest expense	0	0	0	0	0
Cash flow	$100,000	$107,000	$114,490	$122,504	$131,080
Depreciation	55,556	55,556	55,556	55,556	55,556
Taxable income	$ 44,444	$ 51,444	$ 58,934	$ 66,949	$ 75,524

cent inflation rate, it is reasonable that our $1,000,000 building can be sold in five years for $1,400,000. That represents a $400,000 profit which is roughly $80,000 per year. ($400,000 divided by 5 years = $80,000). That is equivalent to about an 8 percent per year return on your $1,000,000 investment. ($80,000 divided by $1,000,000 = 8 percent). The reason 7 percent inflation produces an 8 percent average return is compounding.

Your cash flow started around 10 percent a year and escalated to roughly 13 percent per year, averaging around 11½ percent. Appreciation averaged around 8 percent a year, so the total return is roughly 19½ percent per year.

Tax Advantage of Real Estate

There are also tax advantages. First, look at the tax benefits that affect your yearly cash flow. In the first year, the net operating income was $100,000. However, you will not have to pay tax on the full $100,000. The reason is depreciation. Uncle Sam has allowed most commercial buildings to be depreciated over an 18-year life. (The expected life changes from time to time with new tax legislation.) This simply means that you receive a tax deduction for 1/18th of the purchase price of the building. In the case of a $1,000,000 building, this works out to $55,556 a year. As you can see below and from Table 9–2, you will only be taxed on $44,444 of the $100,000 cash flow.

TABLE 9–2

Gross rents	$150,000
Operating expenses	50,000
Net operating income	$100,000
Depreciation	55,556
Taxable income	44,444
Tax bracket	35%
Tax owed	$ 15,555

What does this mean to your after-tax rate of return if you are in the 35 percent bracket? Since you are taxed only on the $44,444, your tax liability is only $15,555 ($44,444 × 35% = $15,555). The other $55,550 is received tax-free. (Actually you will pay some of it later at long-term capital gains rates.) You keep $84,445 of the $100,000 in income that year. Your after-tax cash return is 8.44 percent.

In a previous section, you learned how to calculate the taxable equivalent; divide 8.44 percent by (1 – .35) or .65, which equals 12.98 percent. To get the same rate of return in a fully taxable investment, like a CD or corporate bond, you would need to receive 12.98 percent. Pretty neat, huh? There's more.

How about tax on those $400,000 in profits? Normally, you would expect to have to pay 35 percent of the profit to Uncle Sam. Fortunately, the IRS gives you a special deal. Because you have held the property longer than six months, it is subject to long-term capital gains treatment. This means that only 40 percent of your profit becomes taxable and 60 percent is tax-free.

To determine how much that is, you must first calculate your taxable profits. Because the IRS allowed you to deduct $55,556 a year in depreciation from your income, it's going to want those deductions back. Over five years, you deducted $277,780 ($55,556 × 5 = $277,780). This amount is now used to reduce your purchase price for the purpose of calculating capital gains. Your purchase price, or cost basis, now becomes $722,220 ($1,000,000 – $277,780). If you sell the property for $1,400,000 and subtract what you paid for tax purposes, $722,220, the IRS says you have a reportable profit of $675,000.

Sales price	$1,400,000
Basis	− 722,220
Taxable profit	$ 677,780

Now calculate the taxes. Only 40 percent of the $677,780 is taxable, or $271,112. Now multiply $271,112 times your tax bracket, 35 percent, to find how much tax you owe, which is only $94,889. Your after-tax profit from appreciation is $305,111.

Actual cash sales price	$1,400,000
Actual cash purchase price	1,000,000
Cash profit	400,000
Taxes owed	94,889
Net profit	$ 305,111

What's the bottom-line result after tax? You're going to have to trust me on this one or we'll be going through numbers all day long. In a 35 percent tax bracket, your after-tax rate of return on this example is 15.52 percent.

Three Benefits of Real Estate

As you can see, there are three major benefits to investment real estate: cash flow, appreciation, and tax shelter. Real estate investments can be structured in order to accentuate some of these benefits and minimize others depending on the needs of the individual investor. The illustration we just went through accentuated the cash flow benefits. It assumed that you paid 100 percent cash for the property. Since we did not borrow any money, we had no interest payments to make. This allows you to keep 100 percent of the net operating income. Table 9–3 illustrates the same property purchased by paying $300,000 down and borrowing $700,000 at 13 percent interest. The net operating income remained the same as Table 9–1, but because of the interest expense of $91,000 per year, the cash flow is reduced to $9,000. That is a 3 percent

TABLE 9-3

	Year 1	Year 2	Year 3	Year 4	Year 5
Rent income	$150,000	$160,500	$171,735	$183,756	$196,619
Expenses	50,000	53,500	57,245	61,252	65,540
Net operating income	$100,000	$107,000	$114,490	$122,504	$131,080
Interest income	91,000	91,000	91,000	91,000	91,000
Cash flow	$ 9,000	$ 16,000	$ 23,490	$ 31,504	$ 40,080
Depreciation	55,556	55,556	55,556	55,556	55,556
Taxable income	($ 46,556)	($ 39,556)	($ 32,066)	($ 24,051)	($ 15,476)

cash return on a $300,000 investment. By the fifth year, you are receiving $40,080 which equals a 13.4 percent cash return on your investment.

In the first year, there is a negative taxable income. This means that you actually receive a tax deduction for $46,556. It can be subtracted from your other income to reduce your overall tax bill. The $9,000 that you receive in cash flow is "sheltered," therefore, not taxable.

Assuming once again that you made a $400,000 profit on the sale of the property, that works out to a 133 percent rate of return for the five-year holding period. It's higher than the previous example because the amount of money invested was only $300,000. That works out to a 26.6 percent average annual appreciation rate. The total after-tax rate of return for the five-year holding period for an investor in the 35 percent tax bracket is 32.03 percent. Table 9-3 offers excellent appreciation potential and tax benefits but little current income.

It looks like Table 9-3 is the place to invest, but don't forget, there ain't no free lunch. When you borrow money to make an investment, you increase the risk of that investment. We assume that the occupancy rate of the building remained at 100 percent. If occupancy rates had dropped much below 95 percent in Table 9-3 there would not have been enough money to pay the interest payment on the loan. If that goes on for very long, the bank will repossess the property and you could lose your entire investment.

Changing the amount of leverage used can change the benefits of the investment. The first example offered a safe stable source of cash flow, some tax benefits, and some appreciation. The second example offered substantial tax benefits, considerable appreciation potential with cash flow being minimized. The second example also involved a great deal more risk.

The retired investor is looking primarily for safety and income. In order to achieve those benefits in real estate, invest in programs that purchase properties for all cash or utilize a minimum amount of borrowing.

Investing in real estate, like investing in common stocks, has risk. It's not like investing in a government bond where you know that eventually you will get all your money back plus interest. The major risk in real estate is keeping the properties leased. If you invest in old property in a bad area, it will be hard to attract tenants. Even investing in new property in a good growth area can be hazardous because of competition. If the area grows too fast, it may become "overbuilt," which means there are not enough tenants to go around. It's possible that you could have an economic condition which causes deflation. In this rare situation, the value of the properties and the rents received may actually go down.

In our examples, we showed that rents increased at a nice even 7 percent rate. In actuality, it never works out quite that way. Some years may see substantial increases; other years may see no increases at all.

Remember, real estate investments are designed to be long-term. Never invest money in real estate that you are going to need in a short time. Real estate needs time to work out, just like the stock market. It does have risks but don't let that deter you. For the retired investor, I would recommend looking at good quality limited partnerships in real estate. They offer you many advantages including the safety of diversification and professional management as well as being a passive investment that requires none of your time.

Remember that growth-oriented investments may need a while to work out. Don't expect to buy them and sell them in the short run. Their primary purpose is to provide you with a long-term hedge against inflation. Select growth investments that are not too volatile and ones with which you are comfortable. Depending on your investment circumstances, you

FIGURE 9–1

Long-Term Growth Mutual Funds

Fidelity Magellan 800-544-6666	Load
Twentieth Century Select 816-531-5575	No load
Dreyfus Third Century 800-645-6561	No load
Templeton Growth Fund 800-237-0738	Load
Growth Fund of America 800-421-9900	Load

Growth and Income—Mutual Fund

Oppenheimer Equity Income 800-221-9839	Load
Pioneer II 800-225-6292	Load
Nueberger & Bernman Guardian 800-367-0770	No load

Real Estate Limited Partnership

Balcor American Express
800-422-5267

Carlyle
800-621-1870

Equitec
800-445-9020

First Capital
312-267-0020

Consolidated Capital
800-227-1870

(Most major brokerage firms also have their own RELPS)

should have as much as 20 percent, but no more than 50 percent, of your assets invested in growth-oriented securities. In Figure 9–1 I have provided a short list of mutual funds that specialize in common stock investments as well as a list of limited partnership syndicators offering real estate limited partnerships.

In the next chapter, we will go back and take a look at Bill and Susan Retiree and how they overcame their long-term investment problem with a few small changes in their investments.

CHAPTER TEN

Practicing What You Have Learned

Now that you have learned it all, let's help Bill and Susan. When we left them in Chapter 5 they had a problem. While they were able to save money today, it looked as if by 1989 they would have to begin spending principal or cut back on their life-style. They can't increase their income except by better investing their money. Table 10–1 is a review of their current situation.

To locate the areas that offer opportunity for improvement, let's review how their investments fit into the five major benefit areas.

Liquidity. Bill and Susan currently have $37,600 invested in highly liquid, low-yielding money markets and savings accounts. This is far too much for their situation. They should close out their savings account and reduce their money market to $7,600. This leaves them plenty of liquidity, equal to almost four months income.

Safety. All their investments are considered safe and any reinvestment program should maintain that same high safety level.

Income. They have $73,500 invested in CDs, EE Bonds, and an IRA. The rate of return on these assets is not as high as it should be. These investments have short-term maturities which means Bill and Susan are sacrificing income.

TABLE 10–1

Current Fixed Income Allocation

	Amount	Rate	Income
CDs	$ 60,000	8.90%	$ 5,340
Savings account	22,000	7.50	1,650
Money market	15,600	7.20	1,123
Government bonds	7,500	8.50	638
Annuities	16,500	11.50	1,897
IRA	6,000	9.20	552
Total	$127,600	8.78%	$11,200

Current Growth Asset Allocation

	Amount	Rate	Income
Common stocks	$ 8,700	5.60%	$ 487
Total	$ 8,700	5.60%	$ 487

Current Income Situation

Pension	$ 4,910
Social security	9,864
Growth income	487
Fixed income	11,200
Total	$26,461

The CD investment should be reduced to $20,000. This amount is sufficient to provide additional liquidity in case of emergency. Despite its low yield of 8.9 percent, there is no risk of principal even if interest rates go up. The EE Bonds offer an inferior yield and should be liquidated. A total of $37,500 should be reinvested in GNMA mortgages. They offer a high 12 percent return and the safety of a U.S. government guarantee. The $6,000 IRA, which is currently in a CD, should be reinvested in a GNMA to produce a higher yield.

Growth. One major reason that Bill and Susan's expenses will exceed their income in just a few years is the lack of growth potential. To provide some growth, they should invest $23,700 in a high-quality common stock mutual fund paying 8 percent in dividends. In addition, another $25,000 should be placed in a real estate limited partnership that

---

TABLE 10–2

Recommended Fixed Income Allocation

	Amount	Rate	Income
CDs	$20,000	8.90%	$ 1,780
Money market	7,600	7.20	547
Government bonds	37,500	12.00	4,500
Annuities	16,500	11.50	1,898
IRA	6,000	12.00	720
Total	$87,600	10.78%	$ 9,445

Recommended Growth Asset Allocation

	Amount	Rate	Income
Common stocks	$23,700	8.00%	$ 1,896
Oil & gas	0	0	0
Real estate	25,000	9.00	2,250
IRA	0	0	0
Total	$48,700	8.51%	$ 4,146

Recommended Income Situation

Earnings	$ 0
Pension	4,910
Social security	9,864
Growth income	4,146
Fixed income	9,445
Total	$28,365

---

purchases property for all cash. This will provide a safe growth investment yielding 9 percent cash flow.

Tax Benefits. Bill and Susan are not in a high enough tax bracket to benefit from additional tax-advantaged investments. Their annuity and IRA allow their investments to compound on a pre-tax basis. The cash flow from the real estate will be partially tax-sheltered. Table 10–2 shows the results of the changes.

A few simple changes can yield dramatic results. Bill and Susan have plenty of liquidity to cover emergencies. This allows them the ability to invest most of their money in long-term fixed-income investments like GNMA. In addition, they now have $48,700 in growth-oriented investments giving them inflation protection. These changes have immediately

TABLE 10–3
Recommended Situation
(inflation rate assumption 5 percent)

Year	Income	Expenses	Savings
1985	$28,365	$19,350	$ 9,015
1986	28,860	20,318	8,543
1987	29,379	21,333	8,046
1988	29,924	22,400	7,524
1989	30,496	23,520	6,976
1990	$31,096	$24,696	$ 6,400
1991	31,727	25,931	5,796
1992	32,389	27,227	5,162
1993	33,086	28,589	4,497
1994	33,819	30,018	3,801
1995	$34,591	$31,519	$ 3,071
1996	35,403	33,095	2,308
1997	36,258	34,750	1,508
1998	37,160	36,487	672
1999	38,110	38,312	(201)
2000	$39,113	$40,227	($ 1,115)
2001	40,171	42,239	(2,068)
2002	41,287	44,351	(3,063)
2003	42,466	46,568	(4,102)
2004	43,712	48,896	(5,185)
2005	$45,028	$51,341	($ 6,313)
2006	46,420	53,908	(7,489)
2007	47,891	56,604	(8,712)
2008	49,448	59,434	(9,986)
2009	51,096	62,406	(11,310)

increased their investment income by $1,904 a year from $11,687 to $13,591.

The real benefit can be seen in Tables 10–3, 10–4, and 10–5. It will now take 10 years, with 7 percent inflation, before Bill and Susan face a problem of expenses exceeding income. During that 10-year period, they will be able to save and reinvest enough so they will not have to invade their original capital for over 20 years. Bill and Susan can now enjoy their retirement with peace of mind. In fact Bill and Susan may have more than enough money to see them through. The next thing they must do is plan for their estate. Chapter 11 will cover some of the essentials of estate planning.

TABLE 10–4
Recommended Situation
(inflation rate assumption 7 percent)

Year	Income	Expenses	Savings
1985	$28,365	$19,350	$ 9,015
1986	29,058	20,705	8,354
1987	29,799	22,154	7,645
1988	30,590	23,705	6,886
1989	31,437	25,364	6,073
1990	$32,343	$27,139	$ 5,204
1991	33,315	29,039	4,276
1992	34,357	31,072	3,285
1993	35,476	33,247	2,229
1994	36,678	35,574	1,104
1995	$37,971	$38,064	($ 94)
1996	39,362	40,729	(1,367)
1997	40,860	43,580	(2,720)
1998	42,475	46,631	(4,155)
1999	44,217	49,895	(5,677)
2000	$46,098	$53,387	($ 7,289)
2001	48,129	57,124	(8,995)
2002	50,325	61,123	(10,798)
2003	52,700	65,402	(12,701)
2004	55,271	69,980	(14,709)
2005	$58,055	$74,878	($16,823)
2006	61,072	80,120	(19,048)
2007	64,343	85,728	(21,385)
2008	67,891	91,729	(23,838)
2009	71,743	98,150	(26,408)

TABLE 10–5
Recommended Situation
(inflation rate assumption 10 percent)

Year	Income	Expenses	Savings
1985	$ 28,365	$ 19,350	$ 9,015
1986	29,355	21,285	8,070
1987	30,442	23,414	7,029
1988	31,636	25,755	5,881
1989	32,951	28,330	4,620
1990	$ 34,400	$ 31,163	$ 3,236
1991	36,001	34,280	1,721
1992	37,772	37,708	64
1993	39,734	41,478	(1,744)
1994	41,912	45,626	(3,714)
1995	$ 44,332	$ 50,189	($ 5,857)
1996	47,026	55,208	(8,181)
1997	50,029	60,729	(10,699)
1998	53,380	66,801	(13,421)
1999	57,124	73,482	(16,357)
2000	$ 61,312	$ 80,830	($19,517)
2001	66,003	88,913	(22,910)
2002	71,262	97,804	(26,542)
2003	77,163	107,584	(30,422)
2004	83,791	118,343	(34,552)
2005	$ 91,242	$130,177	($38,935)
2006	99,626	143,195	(43,568)
2007	109,067	157,514	(48,447)
2008	119,705	173,266	(53,561)
2009	131,700	190,592	(58,892)

SUMMARY

1. Determine your specific investment needs.
2. Dedicate yourself to learning about the investment choices.
3. Diversification is the key to successful investing.
4. Detailed planning is more important than any single investment.

CHAPTER ELEVEN

Estate Planning

If you have done a good job of investing and saving through the retirement years, it is probable that you will leave an estate. The purpose of estate planning is very simple. You decide who gets what, when they receive it, and in what form it will be received. Somebody will receive your assets after you die. It is important that you decide ahead of time who that should be. Without good planning, a large portion of your estate will end up in the hands of the federal government in the form of estate taxes. Another large portion will end up in the hands of your attorneys and the judicial system for probating your estate. By planning ahead, you not only have the opportunity to decide who gets your estate, but you can significantly reduce the amount of it that ends up in taxes and administrative costs.

REDUCING TAXES

Estate and gift taxes are designed specifically to reduce the amount of money that you can give to others. Even with a very modest estate, these taxes can be extremely high. Under current tax law, a tax bill of $23,800 would be due on a taxable estate of just $100,000. On larger estates, the percentage of that estate that goes to taxes increases substantially to over 50 percent.

ESTATE EXPENSES

Taxes are not the only things that reduce the amount you leave to loved ones. It is estimated that the cost of probating and administering the average estate will run between 6 percent and 22 percent of the assets in that estate. This is an awful big chunk to pay attorneys and administrators when, in many cases, it is not necessary. Fortunately, there are a number of things that you can do to substantially reduce the cost of administering your estate. All it takes is a little planning. This chapter on estate planning is not designed to give you tax or legal advice. It will, however, point up some of the mistakes that many people make in planning for the distribution of their estate and how those mistakes might be avoided.

THE ESTATE TAX

One of the major benefits of good estate planning is reducing your estate taxes. The first step in that planning process is to find out how much your estate taxes might be. To do that, it is important to take an inventory of all of your assets that would be taxable in your estate. These assets are more extensive than the inventory that we took in Chapter 3 for your investments. In addition to the assets listed in the Investments section, you would include any life insurance that is payable to your estate, business or partnership interests, any patents or copyrights that you own, and the value of your retirement plans whether they are IRA, pension, or Keogh plans. In addition, you must include all of your personal assets such as automobiles, personal holdings, household goods, jewelry, and so forth. Some assets that you will not need to include are such things as insurance payable to other beneficiaries in which you do not have any ownership or the value of future income that you may receive after your death. The worksheet in the Appendix will help you.

The next step is to value each of the assets. The total of all of these assets is called your gross estate. Fortunately, you do not have to pay tax on this entire amount.

The gross estate can be reduced by several different deductions in order to determine your taxable estate. The taxable estate is the amount on which federal tax tables are applied. These deductions fall into five main categories; debts and liabilities, expenses, federal estate tax credit, contributions made to charity, and marital deduction.

Debts and Liabilities. The first category, debts and liabilities, includes money owed on mortgages, bank loans, unpaid taxes, or other similar debts.

Expenses. These include all funeral expenses as well as the administration expenses of your estate. Included are attorney fees, administrator's commissions, court costs, appraiser's fees, and all other expenses associated with the administration of the estate. Also deductible are any losses in the value of the assets during the administration period to the extent that they are not covered by insurance.

Federal Estate Tax Credit. Occasionally, part of the property has already been taxed in another estate. Under certain circumstances, regulations provide that the second estate does not have to pay the full tax again on that property.

Contributions Made to Charity. Any amounts left to charity in the estate are deducted from the gross estate for the purpose of determining estate taxes.

Marital Deduction. This is probably one of the most important deductions. It includes the value of all property that is passed to a surviving husband or wife. Therefore, all assets that are given to a surviving spouse are not subject to estate tax.

Use the Federal Estate Tax Estimate worksheet in the Appendix to help calculate your taxable estate. After you determine your taxable estate, there is one additional deduction you receive—the unified tax credit.

THE UNIFIED TAX CREDIT

The unified tax credit is a specified amount allowed to be deducted from every estate. To use the unified credit, you

TABLE 11-1
Federal Gift and Estate Tax Rates through 1987

If taxable amount is:				
Over	But Not Over	The Tax Is	Plus	Amount Over
0	$ 10,000	0	18%	0
$ 10,000	20,000	$ 1,800	20	$ 10,000
20,000	40,000	3,800	22	20,000
40,000	60,000	8,200	24	40,000
60,000	80,000	13,000	26	60,000
80,000	100,000	18,200	28	80,000
100,000	150,000	23,800	30	100,000
150,000	250,000	38,800	32	150,000
250,000	500,000	70,800	34	250,000
500,000	750,000	155,800	37	500,000
750,000	1,000,000	248,300	39	750,000
1,000,000	1,250,000	345,800	41	1,000,000
1,250,000	1,500,000	448,300	43	1,250,000
1,500,000	2,000,000	555,800	45	1,500,000
2,000,000	2,500,000	780,800	49	2,000,000
2,500,000	3,000,000	1,025,800	53	2,500,000
3,000,000			55	3,000,000

calculate the amount of the taxable estate and then determine the amount of the taxes owed from the tax table. After you have determined these taxes, you then subtract the amount of the unified tax credit to get the amount of actual tax owed. In 1986, the amount of the unified tax credit is $155,800. In 1987 and thereafter, the amount of the credit for every estate is $192,800.

Sometimes it is easier to think of the unified tax credit as an exemption. Thinking of it that way, it means in 1986 the first $500,000 of a taxable estate will not be subject to tax. In 1987, that goes up to $600,000. Once you have calculated your taxable estate, determine the taxes owed from Table 11-1. Next subtract the unified tax credit to determine the tax due.

Table 11-2 on the next page shows a gross estate of $690,000 and a deduction of $50,000 for funeral expenses, debts, administration, and other expenses.

As you can see, reducing the amount of your taxable estate can be very important. It ensures that the money for which you worked and saved will go to the ones that you

---

TABLE 11–2

Gross estate	$690,000
Less deductions	50,000
Taxable estate	$640,000
Tax (from Table 11–1)	$211,300
Less unified tax credit	– 192,800
Taxes due	$ 18,500

---

love, not to taxes. One simple way of reducing your taxable estate is through gifting.

GIFTING

One of the best ways to reduce the size of your estate is to give the money away before you die. Not only can you substantially reduce the amount of taxes paid on your estate, but you have the opportunity and the joy of seeing those who receive the money benefit from it. Gifting should be considered a total part of your estate planning. It can be very effective in assisting you in accomplishing your personal objectives. It ensures that the people you want to receive your money will receive it, possibly at a time in their lives when they need it most.

There are some important things to consider before you decide to gift. One consideration is taxes. The government has already anticipated that you might use this as a method of escaping estate taxes. Therefore, there is a gift tax. Gift taxes are approximately the same rate as estate taxes. There are four major considerations in the decision as to whether you should make a gift: giving up control, affordability, tax implications, and timing.

Giving Up Control. Once you have given something away, you have given up the right to it and all control over it. This sometimes can be very difficult to deal with psychologically, and the benefits of any tax reduction must be weighed against these considerations.

Can You Afford It?   Naturally, it is impossible to predict exactly what your future income needs might be. Be sure that what you may be giving away won't be needed by you in the future to provide for your own welfare. Very large estates may find it easy to provide for some gifting, but smaller estates must be very careful before assets are given away.

Tax Implications.   Be sure that you determine the tax implications. Will it benefit your estate? What effect will the gift have on the taxes of the person that you are giving it to?

Timing of the Gift.   Achieving your personal objectives is an important part of any gifting program. Gifting may provide you with the opportunity of providing money to your loved ones when they most need it.

SELECTING THE RIGHT PROPERTY TO GIVE

Gifts do not necessarily have to be in the form of cash. When giving property other than cash, there are a number of important tax considerations.

Don't Give Depreciated Property

It is normally not advisable to give property that has dropped below your cost. If the donee (the person receiving the gift) should sell the property, their cost basis for tax purposes is going to be the market value at the time of the gift. Therefore, if the donee sells the property, he or she cannot deduct the lost value of the property for income tax purposes. Any tax deductions that might result from the loss in the value of the asset from your purchase price up to the time the gift is made are gone forever.

It is usually not a good idea to give away appreciated property unless it is given to a charity. If the donee should sell the property after receiving it, the taxable gain is calculated from your original cost basis. The donee will owe tax on the entire capital gain. If the same asset were left in your estate, it would pass to your beneficiaries at a stepped-up cost basis. This means that when they inherit it, they will start with a cost basis for tax purposes established at the time of your death. Therefore, any capital gains that accrue from your cost basis until the time of death would never be taxed.

The only exception might be if you have assets that you expect to appreciate significantly in the future. By gifting this asset before it appreciates, you escape both gift and estate tax on the future appreciation. Another possible exception is when the donee has a much lower tax bracket than yours. If you have an appreciated asset that you have decided to sell, it would be better to gift it to the lower tax bracket donee. When they sell it, they pay the capital gains at a lower rate.

Gifts of income-producing property can also produce an additional tax advantage. If you do not need the income, assets such as fixed-income securities or income-producing real estate can be gifted to family members who are in lower tax brackets. In this way, the income produced by that asset is taxed at their lower tax bracket providing for an income tax savings.

GIFT TAXES

Remember we said that estate taxes are to reduce the amount of assets that are passed from one generation to another. Well, gift taxes are designed to prevent you from avoiding the estate tax.

Taxes on gifts are figured at the same rate as estate taxes (see Table 11–1). These taxes are paid by you on April 15 of the year following the gift. Taxes are paid on the fair market value of the property gifted. Once you reach the point that you must start paying gift taxes, those taxes are cumulative.

THE UNIFIED CREDIT

Each person making a gift has the unified credit that he may use up before having to pay gift taxes. This is the same unified credit that we discussed under estate taxes. In 1986, a donor may give as much as $500,000 without gift taxes. In 1987, that goes to $600,000. Each donor may utilize the full unified credit. This means that a husband and wife in 1987 would be able to give away $1,200,000 ($600,000 each) before incurring any gift taxes. Remember, once you have used up your unified credit in gifting, it is not available to be used against your future estate taxes. There are four kinds of gifts that can be made that completely avoid gift taxes; $10,000 annually, charitable organizations, tuition, and medical.

$10,000 Annually. You can give away as much money as you want without ever being taxed as long as you give no more than $10,000 to any one person in any year. There is no limitation on the number of years this can be done. Each individual donor (the person doing the giving) is allowed $10,000 per year per donee. As an example, this means that a husband and wife can give $10,000 each to each one of their three children every year. Each child can receive $10,000 from his or her father and $10,000 from his or her mother, totaling $20,000. This allows for $60,000 to be given to the children each year.

Charitable Organizations. Any gifts given to charitable organizations are not subject to gift taxes.

Tuition. You may pay the tuition for your children or grandchildren or anyone else you would like without those payments being taxed as gifts. Only tuition is covered under this exemption. Books, room, board, and the like are not considered tax-free gifts. You must make the payments of the tuition directly to the educational institution.

Medical Costs. Direct payments of the medical expenses of another are not subject to gift taxes as long as you make the payments directly to the provider of the medical services.

If you wish to reimburse a family member for the cost of medical care, or for the cost of tuition, that would be considered a taxable gift and subject to gift taxes. The same payment made directly to the educational institution or the medical facility is not considered taxable.

THE GIFT TAX RETURN

IRS Form 709 and 709-A are used to report gifts on an annual basis. These returns are due to the IRS on April 15th of the following year. It is necessary to file the return if charitable gifts of over $10,000 are given. It is necessary to file this form even if the charitable deduction would reduce the taxable gift to zero. It is also necessary to file the return even though the unified credit will completely offset any taxes owed. It is not necessary to file if $10,000 or less is given to each donee, or if the gift is to a spouse qualifying for the unlimited marital deduction.

THE WILL

Any money that you don't spend or give away will be distributed after you die. To be sure that the money is distributed exactly the way you want, you should leave written instructions. These written instructions are included in a legal document called the will.

Should you die without a will, your assets will be distributed by the court. It is highly unlikely that a judge will be able to distribute your assets in exactly the same way that you would have. Many people feel that because they have their assets in joint tenancy with their spouses they don't need a will. This is simply not true. Take for an example the couple who are involved in a serious boating accident. She dies immediately; he dies several weeks later. They didn't have any children, and because there was no will, all of the estate was awarded to his brothers and sisters. The entire estate was considered his. Her family received no benefit of it.

Making Your Will

Because your will is such an important document, you may want to utilize the services of an attorney who specializes in this area. Before sitting down with your attorney, however, there are several important decisions that you must make ahead of time. You must decide how you want your estate divided; who gets what. You may divide your estate up in percentages of the total value, or you may specify that specific assets be distributed to certain beneficiaries, or a combination of the two.

One of the more important decisions you will make is who becomes executor of your estate. Your executor is the one charged with the responsibility of taking care of all of the administrative duties of your estate. In general, an executor is entitled to compensation for these services, and in most states, must post a bond to ensure that they perform the duties adequately. If you are going to name a relative as executor, it would be advisable to allow them to serve without the necessary bond by stating that in your will.

Your will is an important legal document and should be drafted, signed, and witnessed so as to meet all of the requirements of state law. Once you have made up your will, it is not cast in stone but may be changed from time to time. It is probable that you will want to periodically review your will to ensure that it still meets your personal objectives as well as taking maximum advantage of any changes in federal or state tax laws.

If the changes in your will are major ones, you may want to draw up an entirely new document. If, however, the changes are minor, you may make the changes by simply amending the will. This amendment is called a codicil. Be sure, if you do make an amendment to your will, it does not contradict any of the other provisions of the will.

Because of the importance of this legal document, keep it safe and accessible. Many find it convenient to leave a copy of their will with their attorney. Be sure to tell a close friend or relative exactly where your will is kept so that it can be found in a timely manner. A delay of this type could cause substantial inconvenience for your beneficiaries. It is also very practical to keep an unsigned copy of your will at home so that you can refer to it from time to time.

WHY CONSIDER A TRUST

The use of a trust can be an important tool in minimizing your estate taxes. It is also a convenient method of managing assets when the beneficiaries do not have the capability to do so.

Setting up a trust is not complicated. A trust simply transfers the legal title of the specified property and names a trustee who manages the property. The trustee may be one or more persons or a corporation such as a bank or a trust company.

You may create a trust through your will, or you may do so during your lifetime. A trust that is created during your lifetime is called an inter vivos trust. An inter vivos trust may be set up so that the trust can be revoked. In a revocable trust, you retain control over the property by reserving the right to revoke the trust at any time.

THREE PRACTICAL USES OF TRUSTS

There are wide varieties of ways in which trusts can be used. However, there are three primary uses that may be beneficial to most people: asset management, leaving assets to charity, and maximizing the unified credit.

ASSET MANAGEMENT

Often beneficiaries are elderly or incapable through lack of experience of managing the assets they inherit. To ensure that the assets are managed properly, a trust can be set up and a trustee named to take care of the day-to-day management of those assets. The trustee can be a trusted individual or friend, a bank trust department, or a trust company. Having a capable trustee in charge of management of the assets not only ensures that those assets will be managed in accordance with changing economic situations, but also allows that the trust may be managed in such a way as to take care of the changing economic needs of the beneficiaries.

CHARITABLE REMAINDER TRUST

Many individuals wish to leave some portion of their assets to a special charity. This can be accomplished during your lifetime by setting up a charitable remainder trust. When you make the contribution to the trust for the future benefit of the charity, you receive an income tax deduction for that amount. The assets in the trust are usually invested in safe, high-yielding securities. The income from those securities is paid to the grantor (that is the person putting the money in) during his or her lifetime to meet living expenses. After the death of the grantor, the assets revert to the charitable institution.

A husband and wife may wish to set up a trust so that it will pay the income from that trust to them as long as either one of them is living, and then have the assets given to the charitable institution. To illustrate the potential benefit of this trust, assume that after a long career with a major corporation a couple has accumulated a substantial amount of stock in that company, much of it at a very low cost basis. The couple may place the stock in a charitable remainder trust. By doing so, they receive a tax deduction for the market value of the securities at the time that they placed it into the trust. This charitable deduction can be used to reduce the amount of income taxes that they pay in the future. The assets may be sold by the trust and those funds put into high-yield, safe securities such as municipal bonds. In doing so, the trust usually does not have any income taxes to pay on the appreciation if the assets were held long enough to qualify for long-term capital gain treatment. During the lifetime of the couple, the interest received on the bonds in the trust is paid to them. No income taxes are due on the income because the municipal bonds are tax-free. If the investment was made in taxable bonds, the couple would receive the income but they would need to pay income tax on the amount of income received. Upon the death of both spouses, the assets in the trust are paid to the beneficiary which is the charitable organization and are, therefore, not taxed in the estate. Charitable remainder trusts are irrevocable and complex. Be sure you consult an expert to help you draft a trust of this type.

MAXIMIZING THE USE OF THE UNIFIED CREDIT

By utilizing a trust, a couple can maximize the benefit of the unified tax credit available to each one of them. A practical example is as follows. A husband, assuming that he will predecease his wife, sets up his will so that the assets are paid into two trusts, A and B. Trust A is set up so that it qualifies for the marital deduction. Because his wife does not want the responsibility of managing the assets, the trust assets will be managed by an outside money manager. The provisions of Trust A provide that all of the income generated from the trust is paid to her. The trust is designed so that she can change trustees or even dissolve the trust if she wishes. The trust qualifies for the marital deduction so no estate taxes are paid on the amount in Trust A. The assets in Trust A are considered assets of the wife. Upon her death, she may appoint in her will that the assets be paid to her estate or to anyone else she wishes.

Trust B does not qualify for the marital deduction. The amount designated to this trust is equal to the exemption equivalent of the unified credit exemption. After 1987, this is $600,000. Like Trust A, it is managed by a money manager and the income from the trust is paid to the wife during her lifetime. To provide for complete flexibility in the case of unforeseen circumstances, the trustee is given permission to distribute the principal of the trust to provide for the care and welfare of the wife. The assets in Trust B are not assets owned by the wife like they are in Trust A. The assets actually belong to the appointed beneficiaries upon the death of the wife. Trust B provides that upon the death of the wife, the proceeds of the trust are paid to the named beneficiaries, usually the children. The effect of Trust B has allowed both the husband and the wife to utilize the maximum unified tax credit in passing assets on to their heirs while at the same time providing for the health and welfare of the surviving spouse. This technique will save hundreds of thousands of dollars in estate taxes. The illustration below will help explain how.

Assume the total estate upon the death of the husband is $1,200,000. The estate is divided into two parts, Trust A and Trust B. The assets passing to the wife in Trust A are not taxed because of the marital deduction. The assets in Trust B are not taxed because of the utilization of the husband's unified credit deduction.

	Amount	Ownership
Trust A value	$600,000	wife
Less marital deduction	− 600,000	
Taxable	−0−	

	Amount	Ownership
Trust B value	$600,000	Beneficiary after
Less unified credit		death of wife
(husband)	− 600,000	
Taxable	−0−	

Upon the death of the wife, her estate will be passed to her children with no tax consequences as follows:

	Amount
Value of Trust A	$600,000
Less unified credit	
(wife)	− 600,000
Taxable	−0−

The assets in Trust B pass directly to the children and have already been sheltered from tax by the husband's unified credit. In this way, the couple gets the maximum benefit from each unified credit. They pass the entire $1,200,000 to their children free from any inheritance taxes. If they had not utilized the trust, the estate would have passed as follows:

	Amount	Ownership
Assets to wife	$1,200,000	wife
Less marital deduction	− 1,200,000	
Taxable	−0−	

There is no tax when the assets are passed to the wife because of the unlimited marital deduction. After the death of the wife, the assets would be passed to the children as follows:

	Amount
Value of wife's assets	$1,200,000
Less unified credit (wife)	− 600,000
Taxable	$ 600,000
Tax due	$ 192,800

By not planning ahead, $192,800 is lost in taxes.

TAKE SOME TIME

The last illustration was an excellent example of the value of estate planning. After all, $192,000 is a lot of money. Proper estate planning will not only save you money, but it will also ensure that your assets are distributed exactly the way you want. Like everything else that is worthwhile, proper estate planning takes time and energy. The tangible results and peace of mind are well worth the effort. Get started right away by taking an inventory of your assets.

SUMMARY

1. The will is the most important document in estate planning. Be sure that you have one and that it is up-to-date.
2. Gifting can provide an excellent way of reducing estate taxes while allowing you the opportunity to see the benefits of your gift. The charitable remainder trust allows you to make a charitable gift now, receive a current tax deduction, yet still receive the income from the assets to meet living expenses.
3. By the use of trusts, a couple can maximize the benefit of the unified credit to substantially reduce the amount of inheritance taxes they might have to pay.
4. Tax laws change frequently. Be sure you seek the counsel of an attorney who specializes in estate law.

APPENDIX

Sample Planning and Record-Keeping Worksheets

Taxable Property for Estate

Value of:

Stocks _____

Bonds _____

Cash including money markets _____

Real estate owned and mortgages on _____

Annuities _____

Insurance you own _____

Insurance payable to your estate _____

Money owed you _____

Partnerships _____

Some retirement plan benefits _____

Rights to taxable income _____

Personal belongings including cars, furniture, jewelry, etc. _____

Federal Estate Tax Estimate Worksheet

Gross estate   _____

Debts $_____

Administrative expenses
  (approximately 8 percent) $_____

Contributions to charity $_____

Marital deduction $_____

Total deductions   – $_____

Taxable estate   = $_____

Tax due before unified credit   = $_____

Unified credit   – $_____

Total tax due $_____

Income Worksheet

Earned income	$_____
Social security	$_____
Pension	$_____
CDs	$_____
Money market	$_____
Savings account	$_____
Government bonds	$_____
Corporate bonds	$_____
Municipal bonds	$_____
Mortgages	$_____
Annuities	$_____
Preferred stock	$_____
Insurance policies	$_____
IRAs	$_____
Common stocks	$_____
Oil and gas	$_____
Real estate	$_____
Other	$_____
Total	$_____

Budget Worksheet

Rent or mortgage	$_____
Food	$_____
Utilities	
Electricity	$_____
Telephone	$_____
Fuel	$_____
Water	$_____
Clothing	$_____
Transportation	
Auto insurance	$_____
Gas and oil	$_____
Repairs	$_____
Licenses and registrations	$_____
Other	$_____
Insurance	
Home owners	$_____
Life	$_____
Disability	$_____
Medical	$_____
Household expenses	
Laundry	$_____
Garbage	$_____
Maintenance and repairs	$_____
Furnishings and appliances	$_____
Yard maintenance	$_____
Personal care items	$_____
Pets	$_____
Recreation	$_____
Entertainment	$_____
Travel	$_____
Gifts	$_____
Donations	$_____

(Continued)

(Budget worksheet, continued)

Taxes
    Real estate $_____
    Income $_____
    Sales $_____
    Personal property $_____
Loan payments
    Automobile $_____
    Other $_____
    Other $_____
Medical expenses
    Doctor $_____
    Medication $_____
    Dentist $_____
Other $_____
Other $_____

Total expenses $_____

Investment Worksheet

Stocks and Stock Mutual Funds

Shares	Company	Purchase Date	Cost	Ownership	Dividend Income
___	___	___	___	___	___
___	___	___	___	___	___
___	___	___	___	___	___
___	___	___	___	___	___
___	___	___	___	___	___
___	___	___	___	___	___
___	___	___	___	___	___

Bonds (Government—Corporate—Municipal)

Face Amount	Company	Purchase Date	Cost	Ownership	Maturity	Interest Rate	Income
___	___	___	___	___	___	___	___
___	___	___	___	___	___	___	___
___	___	___	___	___	___	___	___
___	___	___	___	___	___	___	___
___	___	___	___	___	___	___	___
___	___	___	___	___	___	___	___
___	___	___	___	___	___	___	___

(Investment worksheet, continued)

Real Estate

Location	Date	Cost	Value	Ownership	Income

Annuities

Amount	Company	Ownership	Beneficiaries	Interest Rate

IRA

Trustee	Type of Investment	Value	Yield

(Investment worksheet, continued)

CDs, Money Funds, Credit Unions, Savings Accounts

Institution	Amount	Maturity	Interest Rate	Income
_____	_____	_____	_____	_____
_____	_____	_____	_____	_____
_____	_____	_____	_____	_____
_____	_____	_____	_____	_____
_____	_____	_____	_____	_____
_____	_____	_____	_____	_____
_____	_____	_____	_____	_____

Checking Accounts

Institution	Amount
_____	_____
_____	_____
_____	_____
_____	_____
_____	_____

Brokerage Accounts

Company	Registered Representative	Account Number
_____	_____	_____
_____	_____	_____
_____	_____	_____
_____	_____	_____
_____	_____	_____

Personal Property Worksheet

Assets	Value
Home furnishings	$________
Automobiles	$________
Furs and clothing	$________
Jewelry	$________
Antiques	$________
Collections	
Art	$________
Coins	$________
Stamps	$________
Other	$________
Copyrights	$________
Patents	$________
Business interests	$________
Other	$________
Total	________

Creditor's Worksheet

Creditor's Name	Maturity	Balance	Amount of Payment
________	________	________	________
________	________	________	________
________	________	________	________
________	________	________	________
________	________	________	________
________	________	________	________
________	________	________	________

Insurance Worksheet

Life Insurance

Amount	Company	Type	Premium	Owner	Beneficiaries
___	___	___	___	___	___
___	___	___	___	___	___
___	___	___	___	___	___
___	___	___	___	___	___
___	___	___	___	___	___

Health Insurance

Company	Coverage	Premium	Agent
___	___	___	___
___	___	___	___
___	___	___	___
___	___	___	___

Disability Insurance

Company	Coverage	Premium	Agent
___	___	___	___
___	___	___	___
___	___	___	___
___	___	___	___

Home Owners Insurance

Company	Coverage	Premium	Agent
___	___	___	___
___	___	___	___
___	___	___	___
___	___	___	___

Worksheet

My Will

I have made a will _____ YES _____ NO

Execution date _____

Location of document

_____

Attorney   Address   Phone

_____   _____   _____

_____   _____   _____

Executor

_____   _____   _____

_____   _____   _____

Last updated   Date _____

Last reviewed   Date _____
(*no changes*)

Beneficiaries

_____

_____

_____

_____

_____

_____

Trust Funds

Trust established for the benefit of:

_____

_____

Date established _____

Location _____

Trustees	Address	Phone
_____	_____	_____
_____	_____	_____

Attorney _____

Asset Manager _____

— —

Trust established for the benefit of:

_____

_____

Date established _____

Location _____

Trustees	Address	Phone
_____	_____	_____
_____	_____	_____

Attorney _____

Asset Manager _____

Advisor Worksheet

Important People

	Name	Address	Phone No.
Personal doctor:			
Attorney:			
Banker:			
Accountant:			
Stockbroker:			
Insurance agent:			
Executor of estate:			
Emergency family contact:			